PAPER TIGER

One Athlete's Journey to the
Underbelly of Pro Football

Ted A. Kluck

THE LYONS PRESS
Guilford, Connecticut
An imprint of The Globe Pequot Press

The Lyons Press is an imprint of The Globe Pequot Press.

10 9 8 7 6 5 4 3 2 1

Printed in the United States of America

Designed by Sheryl P. Kober

Photos courtesy of James Olson

Library of Congress Cataloging-in-Publication Data

Kluck, Ted A.
  Paper tiger : one athlete's journey to the underbelly of pro football/Ted A. Kluck.
    p. cm.
  ISBN-13: 978-1-59921-043-8
1. Kluck, Ted A. 2. Football players--United States. 3. Football—United States—Anecdotes.
4. Football--United States—Humor.
I. Title.
  GV939.K48A3 2007
  796.332092--dc22
  [B]
                              2007008913

For Dad

First and foremost I need to thank Battle Creek Crunch Head Coach Bob Kubiak for the opportunity to take the field with his team every day. I appreciate you, Bob, for taking your football seriously, but also for your well-developed sense of humor and perspective on all of this. Thanks as well to assistant coaches Scott Ashe and Anthony Allsbury, who no doubt had to slow down their drills to pick me up off the artificial turf at times. Ashe, in particular, you are a top-notch teacher of the game in addition to being hilarious. Nobody works harder.

Thanks as well to team owner, Mike Powell, who experienced the wild ups, downs, and regrets of athletics, just as I did. Mike, this book is a sometimes painfully honest account of what happened to you this year but I want you to know that I appreciate you for giving it a shot, and appreciate you having me on board. To the brass at the Great Lakes Indoor Football League—Eric and Jeff Spitaleri, Cory Trapp, and Josh Stein—huge thanks for having the flexibility and vision to allow me to do this. After having worked with many humorless stuffed shirts in many professional leagues, you guys were a breath of fresh air.

To the players, thank you for including me. It was quickly apparent that I was not as fast, strong, or talented as the rest of you, but going to battle with you in practice and on game days was a privilege and I respect all of you for having the courage to play this game well. At the risk of sounding like a high school yearbook inscription, I will never forget you and hope to see some of you playing on Sundays.

Special thanks to Doc Martinez, for the conversations. To Sean, The Intern, for being Sean, The Intern.

To my editor at the Lyons Press, Tom McCarthy, who would have been the quintessential "player's coach." To Bill Stiner, Randy Snow, Jim Olson, and Doc's friend Dana for their great photography. To my agent, Mike O'Brien, for your love of football, and for being principled in an industry full of shysters.

To the friends who sat through games with my wife—Chris and Beth, Ruthie, Ryan and Kel, Detta and Zandy, Anthony and Adrienn—thanks for keeping her company, and thank you even more for your friendship.

To my wife, God bless you for living through another year of football with me. The lonely nights in the stands with Tristan and the long road trips are a sacrifice for you and I fully understand that. As usual, it is your smile, heart, and sense of humor that makes any of this fun in the first place. You are beautiful (more beautiful than the Illegal Motion dancers), and I promise, now for real, that I will never play again. There it is, in writing.

To Gramps for telling me the old football stories over coffee and cigarettes, to Mitch Warner for playing football with me for hours in the field when we were kids, to my high school teammates for making what happened on Friday nights in Hartford City seem bigger than life, and to my mom for always wrapping the wounds with unconditional love.

Finally, to my dad, for all of the hours spent throwing the football together, for all of the long snaps you caught, for all of the weights you lifted with me, for loving God and Mom with all of your heart, and for giving me your time and allowing me full access into your life. This book is yours.

Then, with that faint, fleeting smile playing about his lips, he faced the firing squad; erect and motionless, proud and disdainful, Walter Mitty the Undefeated, inscrutable to the last.

— James Thurber,
The Secret Life of Walter Mitty

The Tryout, 1997

I shouldn't have been surprised, but when you're a kid with a dream you'll do a lot of degrading things on purpose. Like showing up in the wee hours of the morning to an arena in Nashville for one of hundreds of "pro tryout" cattle calls that happen all over the country. The marketing logic is impenetrable—play upon the pride and egos of your community's athletes, charge them sixty bucks a head for the privilege of running a couple of 40s and banging around, and then send them home with sore muscles, bruises, and a T-shirt to show for it. It made no sense but I was twenty-one years old and arena football sounded like a good idea at the time.

So after a six-hour drive to Nashville the previous night, and the confusion of having to explain to my brother and sister-in-law just what it was I was doing in town ("It's arena football, like regular football but indoors on a small field . . . Yes, you get uniforms and a paycheck . . ."), I slammed down a PowerBar and made my way to the Nashville Kats first open tryout. The atrium in front of the arena teemed with athletes and wanna-be athletes—guys wearing college T-shirts, high school T-shirts, or if you were one of the few genetically gifted guys—no T-shirt at all so that all in attendance could stand in awe of your statuesque figure. It was a cross between a fashion show and a gang beat-down.

Everyone had taken pains to pick out the shirt that made them "look big"—a very important part of sports culture. Although you would never own up to caring about fashion, you spend more time than a high school girl on prom night, standing in front of the closet picking out the right outfit. You want to get noticed but not stick out, because, at its heart, football is still about conformity.

You are herded through huge glass double doors where you fill out an "information sheet" about your exploits as a football player. You lie about your height and weight. You are fifteen pounds heavier and an inch taller. You don't feel bad because everybody does it. You pay the sixty bucks and get a "Nashville Kats" T-shirt with a number pinned to the back. Buyer's remorse sets in. You do a little quick math and realize that you will drop more than a hundred bucks on this trip before it's all said and done. You feel like a sucker.

You sit down on the field to stretch, feeling the Astroturf scratch and tickle your hamstrings. Your head pivots around in all directions, sizing up the fresh new arena and all of the two hundred other men in attendance. The team will keep two of you. Your ego at this point is big enough not to care. You sit down to stretch with a kid who played some college ball at Louisville.

"How much do you bench?" he asks.

This is the football version of "what's your sign." The most oft-used opening line in the business. You tell him. You lie and add on a few pounds because this kid won't know the difference.

"I did twenty-five reps at 225 in training," he replies, explaining his prowess in the most standard of all football tests.

"Great—glad to hear it." You don't want to talk to him anymore and wish he would beat it, but you are actually glad to not be sitting there by yourself, so you hear yourself asking: "Are we gonna bench today . . . is it just running . . . are we gonna do any team stuff?" You are rambling. You are showing your nerves.

"I dunno. I heard benching. I heard the cone drill. Agilities. Running. Some team stuff. I dunno." He is nervous, too. Good.

You are weighed and measured and you appear shorter and lighter than when you weighed in at home a couple of days ago. You measure 6-foot-2 and 212 pounds. At least 20 pounds too small to play fullback and linebacker in the arena league and 30 pounds lighter than you were in college. You should grab your stuff and go home but delusion keeps you there. Your college education goes out the window at this point, as does any sense of logic.

Your right hand is planted in the turf and your left hand is perched above your left hip. You are in the starting position for the 40-yard sprint, also known as the great eliminator. If you are a tenth too slow you can pack your things and go home. You are free to go when you are ready, because the computer will start timing when your hand comes off the carpet. High tech. You thank God they don't tell you your time because you felt a little slow and probably were. You are breathing heavily not from exertion but from excitement.

The head coach, Eddie Khayat, stands off to the side chomping on a cigar that looks like a giant, gnarled turd. He has that pallid, gray look of a guy who has smoked cigars all his life. He is tall and paunchy and bored looking. He played a little offensive line in the League back in the fifties. He looks like he would rather be anywhere but here. Maybe he is thinking about a party from last night or the tax return paperwork on his credenza at home. You wish he would try harder to conceal the fact that he's not paying attention.

You move to the cone drill and promptly sprain your ankle. Some kid with a team polo on wraps it in tape and asks if you plan to continue.

"Of course," you reply. You don't want to look like a wus, and you drove six hours for crying out loud. The TV crew just got here. They want you to "bounce up and down like you're warming up." You comply and look foolish. It will appear on the evening news, which you will not see because you will be in a car headed for home.

You limp through some halfhearted agility drills led by a defensive line coach with big muscles and thinning hair named Sperduto, whose enthusiasm is in stark contrast to Khayat's cadaver impersonation. He yells, he screams, you feel better. The ankle is coming around. Out of the corner of your eye you spot "Mr. Wonderful Paul Orndorff" the wrestler from the eighties. "What in the world is he doing here?" you half mumble to yourself. He is wearing those bright Zubaz pants that were popular about twelve years ago. He is fake baked to within an inch of his life and looks like a piece of beef jerky. "What is he doing here?" you wonder again. Then again, what am I doing here?

It's almost time for one-on-one drills. You are first in line for one-on-ones because it is a pride thing to be first. You think that even though you are undersized and slow the coaches will like you because you have gone first. You have done it this way your whole life and it is a source of pride, however small. You are paired off against some guy with Steelers shorts and a mesh jersey on. You wonder if he was in their camp. His muscles are huge. He is a blitzing linebacker and it is your job to block him from the fullback position. You block him, you hold your own and your confidence soars as you get back in line. This is fun. This is football. The six-hour drive suddenly seems not so bad and the sixty bucks is a bargain at twice the price. You cycle back through several times—getting straight-up freight-trained once, which leaves you hurting and turf burned. You bang heads with a different kid who also played at Louisville. You stick your hand up in your hair and feel blood. It will be about seven hours before you get home and your wife can clean it up for you.

The drills end anticlimactically and you just want to get out of there. Khayat mumbles something about pride and leads you and the group of strangers through a lame cheer (K-A-T-S. Kats, Kats, Kats!). They'll get in touch with the guys they want to see again (probably nobody). Don't call us—we'll call you. You and your sore ankle wait around for a minute to see if any coaches show interest and then you bound up the stairs to the car. You drive home . . . for six long, boring, painful hours in which you would like to say you did a lot of soul searching and learned a great deal about your character but you actually just stare out the window like a zombie and listen to music . . . praying to God that you will be home soon. You don't even stop for dinner.

Your wife meets you at the door. "How did it go?" she asks.

Your lower lip quivers.

Chapter One

Dispatches
from Week Two

I should have left it alone. That's it. That's the theme, if you believe in themes, of this whole experience, not only for myself but for a lot of guys on the team (the Battle Creek Crunch of the Great Lakes Indoor Football League) who you'll get to know later. After winning my long-snapping job back during the week I ended up getting yanked again, but this time not because of bad snaps but because I was getting run over by people much larger than I am (I have the turf burns to prove it—the inventor of Astroturf should be stripped naked and dragged across his invention for an hour or so). They decided they wanted a bigger body in there to hold the line after the snaps. Can't argue with that . . .

This whole thing has been a big roller coaster of emotions . . . God is showing me a lot of things about myself, which, I suppose, is good. But, to be honest, I'm sick of building character.

It has been cool just to be a part of pro football in the little ways—the crowd, the arena, the music, the warm-ups, the autographs, getting my licks in out on the field. The feel of the rough grains of the leather football against your arm as you take a handoff and turn up field. But I am discovering that I can't really do this anymore. I'm not as good as I was five years ago, and I wasn't even that good then. But on my better days I realize just what a coup it is to be out there . . . how the victory was just in getting this to happen. But yeah, it sucks to be a part of a losing team again. In fact, I've never been a part of a winning team, except for one year, my first year in semipro with the Delaware County Thunder after which I should have just left it alone. But I'm learning that the ability to leave it alone is not something that most athletes possess. That's why fighters fight too long, and that's why the majority of the guys I'm playing with now are still playing. It's why I'm on a bad team again.

The locker room is basically empty now because most of the guys are out on the field signing autographs. Autographs are a tough call because on the one hand it's fun to be made much of by fans, and really makes all of the crap we go through worthwhile, but on the other hand I feel like if people really knew how I played tonight and what I was, (a writer masquerading as a professional athlete) they wouldn't want anything to do with my signature on their T-shirt, program, or football. So I have the rare experience of having the dressing room to myself.

It's tiny. Cramped. Not enough chairs and not enough space to go around. I see the vestiges of the game all around me. Tape wadded up on the floor. Discarded shoulder pads and helmets. Special teams lists scrawled on the greaseboard. A mirror, so the guys can check out their uniforms before the game (a little secret, we're all incredibly vain). Soon, Head Coach Bob Kubiak will be in to rant at us for blowing the game. He will blame (though, he says, he's not blaming anyone for the loss) the kicking game (we lost by three points, he says, you do the math) for the loss and I, as the long snapper, am a crucial part of the kicking game. This makes me want to crawl into a hole and die, my already obvious credibility issues notwithstanding. What was once cool—having an ESPN writer and book author with the team—has probably now become a nuisance. I think about how if we had managed to squeeze out three more points, everybody would be best pals and everything would be cool on this night. But as it stands, everybody is pissed at everybody and I have a huge, bloody turf burn on my left arm, which I need to cover before slipping back into the dress shirt I wore to the arena tonight.

There have already been wholesale roster changes, and there were several players who signed their first pro contract just minutes before the game tonight. I didn't even know their names. Some of them will be gone next week and some will still be around. We have a bye next week, and then a nine-hour bus ride to Rochester to face the best team in the league. I'm already dreading it beyond belief. And it's only week two.

Chapter Two

Semipro, 1999–2001

Don't think too much, you'll hurt the ball club.

—Crash Davis, *Bull Durham*

Earl Parsons was an unshaven thirty-eight-year-old in a Bermuda shirt who appeared in my office in 1999 with "official team documents," that when signed, would make me a member of the Delaware County Thunder semipro football club. He looked like a guy who represented a certain absence of responsibility—with his receding hairline, gold medallions, and crusty chest hair—the kind of guy who was fighting middle age with both fists and probably had a Camaro or some other such Midlife Crisis Machine parked out front. From where I was sitting, in a pair of Dockers, a boring golf shirt, and six months into my first "real" job, nothing seemed more appealing.

I would later learn that Earl had an MBA and had played collegiately at the University of Tennessee, but that his hours were whiled away in the gym or breaking down game tapes in his small apartment. He had dated the same girl for seventeen years, and I always told him to "wait it out" because you really don't know someone until you've been together for at least eighteen. At which point he would laugh and tell me to go screw myself. Earl was the world's oldest adolescent. His girl never missed a game, and even wore his jersey (number 10) in the stands. It was sweet and ridiculous at the same time. It was a stupid drug, but I wanted some.

He invited me to suit up for a game the next day, having not a minute of practice to my name. I politely declined but said I was excited to go to practice and see where I stood. I could feel my heart beat in my chest again and in my mind I was already a warrior rather than a slob in a cubicle. I immediately phoned my dad and told him I was a ballplayer again. He was worried sick but didn't want to miss my first game.

I signed my "contract" that afternoon—a hastily drawn document mimeographed onto orange paper. It was less a contract and more an agreement that I wouldn't sue the team for all it was worth (not much) if I happened to break my neck.

"Make no mistake about it," Earl explained as he left, "I run this ball club."

Two weeks later he would throw me the first touchdown pass of the rest of my life. I was back.

Fast forward to the year 2001. Semipro football is a bad virus that won't go away. Each and every spring it comes back and nags at me until I join a team and put my quickly deteriorating body in the path of angry, drug-laced ex-cons, factory workers, has-beens, and never-weres. I tell friends that "everyone takes risks in different ways—this is my way of expressing myself." Then I run down the litany of things I don't do: drugs . . . riding a motorcy-cle . . . skydiving . . . It is psychobabble, admittedly, because play-ing semipro (adult, full-contact) football at my age is simply a bad idea and evidence of poor judgment. While my friends are trading stocks online and cranking out perfect children, I scour pawn-shops for a new helmet and set of shoulder pads. It is an addic-tion. A sickness.

I am twenty-five years old—an age when clerks and waitresses no longer think I'm in college, when I no longer get carded at bars, and when my in-laws no longer think that a small studio apartment is charming and expect better for their daughter. My friends don't want to pay seven bucks to sit in a crappy high school stadium and watch me play football. I am now expected to earn and be obsessed by the pursuit of money and professional advancement, and when I'm not at work, I should be hovering over an overpriced imported lager, discussing what kind of house I'm going to build and what kind of car I will drive. The really important things in life.

I survived the first practice of the season on Saturday, although I feel like I've been in a car accident, and the entire left side of my body from shoulder to wrist is purple. I feel okay as long as I'm not moving or laughing or breathing or lying on that side of my body. Nonetheless, I'm already feeling harder—harder than the other guys in the office and harder than I felt the day before. I feel like I have gone to war and come out stronger. I have lived. I'm also beginning to sound a little melodramatic—like I was weaned on NFL Films and told bedtime stories by John Facenda. I should wake up. Get real. I have dishes to do for the love of God. Bills to pay. Cat to feed. Whatever.

I arrived about a half hour early to practice and stood outside the stadium shuffling uncomfortably with about six other new guys who, like I, were trying to look tough (puff out chest, wear short sleeves when it's like twenty degrees out). There was little chatter beyond talking in octaves-lower tones about our previous football careers—stuff like: "I played for this guy at this school . . . blah blah blah. I was so nervous I went to the bathroom three times in the hour before practice. I have lived in a third-world country, interviewed heavyweight champions, and have been alive for twenty-five years yet I have never been so nervous as before a football practice or game. It's an experience like no other and the reality that you will soon be throwing your body with malicious intent against the men you are talking to about work and kids makes it all the more real. But I feel like I've found an old friend in my shoulder pads. They insulate me from reality—my job, my cubicle, the stack of bills on my credenza at home.

Soon the coaches arrived, talking in hoarse, coach-voices and barking at us like the emotionally underdeveloped human cattle that they must know we are. They were comfortingly typical: middle-aged, paunchy, chomping a huge chaw of tobacco (required), and spouting dockworker vocabulary ("We're going to open some f'ing holes today boys!"). Soon they had herded us through the fence and on to an Astroturf field that resembled green sandpaper pulled over a slab of concrete.

The veterans laughed out loud and told lewd stories in their small cliques as only veterans can. They told of late night, booze-soaked carousings with nameless, faceless, overweight Midwestern girls in a way that made them seem like movie starlets. And in a way that made their veteran womb seem very warm and appealing. They were loopy and wore ball caps and acted very differently than they do while stamping out transmission parts at BorgWarner or processing insurance claims for Jackson National Life. In this arena, they had arrived. Meanwhile, I stood on the outside as only a rookie can. The raw, cold air of the Michigan pseudo-spring filled my nostrils.

And froze my fingers, which is a bad scenario for a tight end whose job it is to catch the ball. I breathed furiously into my gloved hands while waiting in line for a drill called the "Oklahoma" which pits two players 5 yards apart who, at the crack of a whistle, barrel into each other at full speed. The coach explained that in the preseason it is necessary to "build your bruises," and although I questioned the medical validity of his theory, I readied myself for the drill. I partook of the Oklahoma drill as surreal scenes of old football movies played in my head: *Paper Lion*, *The Program*, *Any Given Sunday*. I was mentally comparing my present carnage with the carnage presented in movies. What in God's name am I doing? The Oklahoma ended well—I didn't dominate anyone but I certainly wasn't dominated.

After pass routes (a few drops, one nice catch) and a scrimmage (one killer drive block that I hope someone saw) it was back in the sedan for the lonely ride home to a beautiful young woman who won't quite get it. I'll tell her what I did and in her sweet way she'll not really understand the pleasure I get from punishing my body.

She'll suggest a movie. We'll grab dinner and talk about grownup things. Maybe if I'm lucky she'll sit me down on the cold toilet seat, swab out my cuts and turf burns as if I'm some kind of sado-masochistic returning hero, and then it will lead to something. Or maybe it won't because after performing on the field I might be too tired to perform where it counts.

I gulped water and thought about nothing at all. I was experiencing total exhaustion. If I could bottle and sell the feeling I'm fairly certain I would never work again. I parked the car and walked into my house still wearing the football pants; hoping someone would notice and ask me where I'd been.

Nobody said a word.

It's odd how someone can change the course of your life completely and you might not know him or even learn his name. That's the way it was with the guy who broke my collarbone in two and started the first day of the rest of my life. It was a routine out pattern—I dive for a pass, which I catch, and get up to run with the football, because our semipro league plays with NFL rules.

As I turn upfield I am immediately blasted by a red-and-black-clad defensive back from the Detroit Renegades. He flies up and hits me like a missile—a sensation that, oddly enough, feels almost detached and blissful. It's like riding a ride at the county fair—you just hold on for dear life and hope you don't fall out. Getting blown up on a football field is much the same. I absorb the hit and fall onto my right shoulder, and have the experience of once again hearing one of my bones snap and being confronted with my own mortality. I cradle the ball in my right hand and pop up off the turf as though nothing has happened, although it feels as if someone's holding a cigarette lighter to my shoulder that's slowly burning a hole through my flesh and down farther into my bones. I suffer through the next play call in the huddle—it's a reverse—a play that calls for me to hold my block on the outside linebacker for several seconds. It will be impossible because my arm hangs limply at my side. I tell no one. By this point, I know my game, and probably my sorry excuse for a career, is over, but I manage to trudge over and collapse into my stance—praying to God with all of my being that no one hits me and I can walk off the field with my dignity and my shoulder intact. I also remember to thank Him that I haven't broken my neck.

I always figured it would come to this, actually, and not just in that overly dramatic, melancholy writer sort of way. I figured it would take the most tragic, horrific experience to actually get me to quit playing, to quit feeling the ache every fall. I would need to hate football to the core of my being in order to quit loving it, and thereby wasting my life on it. I figured there would be no in between. But I think this might do the trick.

After the reverse—we score by the way—I make it to the sidelines where I freak out because I can't even get out of my own pads. I roll around on the ground for a while, in front of the crowd and my teammates who haven't a clue what to do. My shoulder burns with pain, and a number of teammates compliment me on the catch. As I sit there on the ground I catch the eye of the DB who planted me into the turf. A black guy, wearing lots of bandannas and stuff. (I think he was number 9 but I'm not sure; it's already fading.) He looks over and asks me if I'm okay. I say yes because it's football, and that's all you can say. I appreciate it, I really do. I don't hate him. I don't even know him. He'll go into the factory tomorrow and I'll go to the doctor to get pills and a sling. Could have easily been the other way around. Life is funny that way. I guess this is what I needed.

I momentarily ponder the indignity of the whole thing—breaking a bone in a game that means nothing on a piddly high school field. I feel sorry for myself for a few minutes before deciding I need to call my wife.

"Honey, it's me."

"What's wrong?"

"I got hurt."

"I know, baby. How bad is it?"

"Just my shoulder. I think I broke my collarbone." My mouth is so dry I can barely get the words out. And the cell phone gives the impression of talking in the middle of a static storm. I look up in the stands and watch people watching me. It is an odd sensation.

"Oh, thank God."

"Can you come get me? I'm sorry, baby. I'm so sorry." And I flip the phone shut, prepared to resume the work of getting out of my pads. A coach saunters over.

"Wife didn't want you playing, huh?"

"No, I guess not."

"Well, that's why I'm coaching and not playing, heh, heh."

Nice. What a class act, this guy.

They proceed to cut off my jersey and pads, and I can finally breathe and see the huge knot forming on my shoulder. I walk out of the stadium as the wives, children, and girlfriends gawk. It sucks to see somebody hurt—kind of ruins the whole vibe. Some little kid carries my pads into the empty locker room for me. I wonder if it gives him a thrill. It would have me, at that age. I wanted nothing more than to be around football and football players, but now I just want my mother. It's funny how at twenty-six you can go from beating the tar out of some guy to wanting your mother in a matter of minutes.

The next twenty minutes are among the longest in my life.

I sit by myself in a locker room off to the side of the playing field. It's a typical room—decorated in a charming gray, cinderblock institutional style. I spend the time trying very hard not to hyperventilate. I hold a leaky bag of ice to my shoulder for a few minutes but feel a little foolish. When you have a broken bone, ice is a joke. My body almost seems to be laughing at it—as if to say that the damage had already been done. Occasionally, I hear the roar of the small crowd as something exciting happens on the field.

I would like to say that I heroically dragged myself out to the sidelines to be with my comrades as they went to war. But I knew I was finished as a member of the Lansing Lightning at the precise moment I heard my clavicle snap in two. I played the last play for reasons unknown even to myself. I pace the locker room and listen to my plastic cleats clacking against the hard concrete floor. It's a sound I realize I will never hear again. I walk by the mirror in the tunnel leading to the field. An hour before I had walked by it in my helmet—impressed at the image of the tough guy in the mirror. Now I walk by shirtless, hair mussed and eyes bloodshot, as an ugly purple welt raises up from my shoulder. I realize that I won't be lifting weights for a while. I realize that I probably won't be going to the beach with my friends the next day as planned. Depression sets in. I begin to worry about whether they will charge my wife the price of admission for the right to come and collect her broken-down husband.

I move to a bench outside the locker room and see her approach the ticket booth and walk right by, uninhibited. She's wearing Capri pants and a nice tank top with a sun hat and glasses. She looks like she's ready to go to the beach. I immediately begin to cry.

"Hi, baby. Thanks for coming."

She collects me in her arms, careless of the sweat and grime that I have accumulated over the course of the afternoon.

I begin apologizing profusely for the inconvenience this will cause—everything from ruining our social plans, to having to shave with my left hand, to not being able to mow the lawn.

I am shockingly thorough and unrelenting in my worry.

She smiles, picks up my gear, and cries a few tears of joy—because she knows it is over.

"C'mon. Let's get out of here."

Chapter Three

The Spirit of the Thing, Present Day

Here's to one more summer in the sun.

—Jake Taylor, *Major League*

It started as small snippets of conversation with her, think of them as little warning shots flared above the horizon of our young marriage. I am nearly thirty now and already the veteran of a handful of unsatisfying careers—junk mail copywriter, university fund-raiser, among others. But this one I like. First book on the shelves, magazine projects underway. I worked on my pitch to her as a top salesman would the day before making the presentation to the Big Company. Lines were rehearsed through shaving cream in front of a bathroom mirror. This will be the toughest sales job of my life, I know, persuading her to let me play again. I thought we were done with all of this, she would say. I thought you got this out of your system a few years ago when, playing semipro, you broke your collarbone and spent an evening in a drab city hospital, the overweight, effeminate doctor lecturing you in a tiny exam room about the dangers of playing semipro football. "Take two of these, every four hours," he said, "and wear this brace until the bone heals."

I had surgery three weeks later. She bought me a recliner in which to convalesce. My friend Billy Yang brought me a stack of football magazines for which I thanked him profusely and then refused to look at because I was done with football and hated it. I had turned a corner. "Don't ever let me do that again," I told her, as I came to in the recovery room sick with nausea, drainage tubes sticking out of the various wounds.

I knew she would use that against me.

Don't get me wrong, I'm not the first writer to work out my masculinity with fear and trembling by putting my body in the way of physical harm. Hemingway brawled and danced with the bulls and Plimpton put on the helmet, the goalie's kit, and the pugilist's gloves—embarrassing himself along the way but leaving behind a trail of blood and premium reading. And Mailer, by letting himself be cuffed about in the ring by pros and amateurs alike, gave us some of the best boxing writing to ever touch the page. Sadly, Mailer the man almost seemed at his most comfortable and effective when he was hitting or being hit.

Sad, but not all that uncommon really.

Football isn't necessarily a bad thing. Sure, once in a while I succumb to a moment of weakness—a moment of Vermont, blue-state, "football is damaging to a young man's psyche" type of weakness. It's the kind of weakness that makes you want to start doing yoga, teach your kid soccer, or order the gardenburger. You pull out that old Dave Meggysey book called *Out of Their League* that talks about hippie rebels who walked away in their prime. You talk about how much you don't miss it, you're over it, and you've grown out of it. You're finally going to focus on your career. Make some real money. Sort some things out.

And then it goes away, as quickly as it came. The Metallica albums come out of a box in the attic. Weights in the basement get lifted. Internet sites are searched and e-mails to coaches are sent. Equipment is purchased. Wife persuaded.

Mike Powell stood out from the semipro crowd for a couple of reasons—one, he was about ten years older than everyone else when we both played for Michigan's Jackson Bombers, a semipro outfit known for its deep pool of talent and yearly runs to the national semipro playoffs.

I knew Powell worked in a white-collar job . . . investments or insurance or something, but I never really discerned what, nor did I know him well when we were with Jackson. He also didn't fit into any of the familiar semipro categories of "recently released from prison" or "looking to move to the next level," rather, like me, he was just a guy playing football because he probably didn't know how to stop playing football. Our paths rarely crossed and our interactions were limited to the typical football "what's up" kind of banter. Needless to say, I was surprised to see that he was an owner of a new professional indoor football team, in a new league (the Great Lakes Indoor Football League).

I drove to Powell's office in Battle Creek, fully expecting to be told "no" because, as a writer, bracing oneself for being told no is a self-preservatory maneuver necessary for living in this business where "no" is a way of life. Powell's office was located in a nondescript bank building (white, one-story, drive-up ATM) in a nondescript section of Battle Creek. I entered, finding a hastily scrawled note about the Battle Creek Crunch and an arrow on a grease board near the entrance to the bank.

My pitch was simple, to convince Powell to allow a writer to be a contributing member of his team for a season, chronicling the experience in a series of columns on ESPN.com and a forthcoming (this) book project. In truth, neither were set in stone. I had an e-mail from editors at both ESPN and the Lyons Press, saying that the project sounded interesting, but no contracts in hand. I gathered that the writing people were waiting for a commitment from the football people, while the football people were waiting on a commitment from the writing people. It was a classic case of who would blink first.

Powell was friendly and we spent a moment rehashing our various semipro experiences, which for me, now, seemed very far away. I was now a father, and caravanning to various ghetto middle schools for practices and games was the last thing on my mind. I didn't even "dress big" for the meeting—meaning that I didn't wear the outfit that made me look the biggest and most menacing in person. I wore the same jeans, T-shirt, and black dark-frame "smart" glasses that all of the writers and pseudo-hipsters were wearing. I had with me a traveling portfolio containing clips, and a sample of what my first book, *Facing Tyson*, would look like when it hit the shelves. This, I had hoped, would build credibility.

Powell's office put me at ease. There were proofs of his day job all around—brochures featuring silver-haired white folks dressed in pastel sweaters on such topics as building financial freedom, life insurance, and investing. It was a working space—not one of the swank, huge offices with snifters of brandy that people get when they no longer have to do any real work. He was often interrupted by cellphone calls (ringtone: the *Monday Night Football* intro song), answering various questions about team offices (being painted as we speak by semipro football players), uniforms, arena, and the like. I see pictures of a family on top of a file cabinet and wonder what they think of this endeavor that will no doubt take their husband and father away from them for long periods of time so that he can worry about such things as practice jerseys and lining the game field by hand. Like alcoholism, football is an addiction that trickles down to friends and family . . . there are dinner parties, holiday gatherings, and various otherwise normal activities missed in the pursuit of the buzz.

This is the kind of self-reflection that can kill a football career, though, and I am snapped back to reality when Powell, after some digging in a briefcase, produces a mock-up of the team uniform and field design as they will appear in Kellogg Arena. We both sit silently in front of the sheet of paper for a moment: Powell, drunk on the realization that he owns a professional ball club, and me, realizing that I will be wearing a uniform again. I shake Powell's hand and drive home, deciding how I will break the news to my wife that I will be a professional football player. Not a bad problem to have. Not bad at all.

I'm just trying to capture the spirit of the thing.

—the great sportswriter Dickie Dunn, in *Slap Shot*

At least that's what I told myself, and what I told my wife when she reminded me that it's not my body that's the commodity, but my mind. And while Dunn was a little pathetic for trying to buddy up to the athletes, at least he wasn't trying to be one.

I am twenty-nine years old, and a long time ago I identified myself as a football player. In retrospect, there is a lot wrong with that—limiting oneself to an identity forged on playgrounds and in weight rooms isn't the right way to go. But neither is real life, with its bills, taupe houses, and pretense, which is what years twenty-two through twenty-nine have shown me. It's still better to be out on the field, pulling a hammy, than it is to be the guy with the tape recorder asking the athlete how he is feeling.

Hence, this project, this day, and this tryout.

This is why I'm stretching on a swath of FieldTurf (feels nice, kinda spongy, like real grass with little chunks of rubber between the blades), getting ready to run a 40-yard dash, a short shuttle (sometimes called the "Jangle") and square off against other guys with a fifty-dollar tryout fee and a dream. The dream, in this case, is to earn a place on the bottom of the professional indoor football food chain—a spot with the Battle Creek Crunch of the Great Lakes Indoor Football League. While my buddies spend their Saturday afternoons at Home Depot picking out marble countertops, I'm about to see how many times I can lift 225 pounds off my chest.

The tryout will be conducted at a place called the Kingdom Indoor Center—an indoor soccer and rec facility nestled into Kalamazoo's south-side industrial district next to a number of soul-sucking office parks and past a handful of the usual chain restaurants. The Center is one of millions like it—a pole barn–like building full of a handful of Astroturf fields, a bunch of privileged kids running around after a soccer ball, and parents in sweaters standing admiringly around the field, worshipping their progeny. Just driving to the place reminds us of what we don't want to go back to, which is being ordinary guys with ordinary jobs. Today is a stab at being "special."

The Great Lakes Indoor Football League is the brainchild of two entrepreneurial brothers from Canton, Ohio, the city that hosted the meetings that resulted in the formation of the NFL in 1920. The GLIFL, in its inaugural season in 2006, will feature seven-on-seven football played indoors on a 50-yard field, with teams in Battle Creek and Port Huron, Michigan; Marion, Ohio; Lehigh Valley, Pennsylvania; Rochester, New York; as well as a team in "TBD," New Jersey. It is a brand of football that has sold well in small to midsized cities across the country—fans can see real, live, violent pro football, for a fraction of the cost of the NFL experience. The league also hopes to serve as a launchpad for many great athletes who, by nature of the numbers game, don't have the opportunity to ply their trade on the NFL stage. There are several of them here, as well as some on the other side of the fence—middle-agers or office workers looking for one more thrill. But nobody is getting rich. My agent, Mike O'Brien, who is in the process of recruiting first-round prospects for this year's NFL draft, will make a commission of three dollars per game on me (the Crunch have guaranteed me a spot on the roster as a long snapper and reserve linebacker and running back)—not quite enough for a hot dog and a Coke at Kellogg Arena.

After walking into the half-dark facility I realize that, true to form, I am about forty-five minutes early and nobody is here. This hyperpunctuality is a product of nerves for me. I feel like if I show up to places early I can stave off any problems that might arise— problems like being too small and too slow notwithstanding. I take up residence along the edge of the Astroturf, about 35 yards away from a group of football-looking (shaved heads, thick chests, sweatpants) guys standing in the middle of the field. If I had to guess I would say they are coaches, and, me being the ESPN writer here on assignment I should feel comfortable going to chat them up. Instead, I stay cemented to the edge of the turf, until a tall guy with the requisite coach-limp sidles by. I introduce myself and learn that he is Bob Kubiak, the head coach, and that he is damn glad to meet me and glad that I will be on board this year. Kubiak has ruddy skin and a friendly face. He calls me "Paper Lion" and genuinely puts me at ease before limping away to deal with a problem. Great. Mission accomplished. Coach met. I strongly consider avoiding embarrassment by putting my little body in my little car (Toyota Echo) and driving home.

Finally, the players begin to trickle in. The key to the tryout seems to be to look as big as possible. There is lots of Under Armour in the room, which, if worn in the privacy of one's home, makes one feel like Superman—an effect that completely wears off in the presence of great athletes. They ought to put that on a warning label. And there are lots of great athletes here. You know them—they're the guys who don't look nervous, not even a bit. When they jog, when they toss a ball, when they talk . . . they make everything look easy.

One of those athletes is Cullen Davis, a lanky, twenty-six-year-old semipro wide receiver who matriculated, in his words, "at the school of hard knocks." Davis can run and catch, but he's one of the many who have fallen through the cracks. There are linemen here from the University of Toledo. A fullback from Michigan State. And a quarterback, Ken Kubiak (Bob's brother—more on that later), thirty-nine, who hasn't played organized football since 1992, when he played for a semipro outfit called the Lansing Crusaders.

"As a coach, I'm always throwing to my kids anyway on the practice field," Kubiak says. "So I guess I never really stopped playing."

Another player puts Kubiak's age in a different perspective: "I think that quarterback was my eighth-grade gym teacher," he says, without a hint of irony.

Personalities reveal themselves in my group of running backs and linebackers. There is the nervous talker. The cocky guy. The guy with the injury that he uses as an excuse for his performance in every drill (this guy is also the nervous talker). I have already developed a nickname: "ESPN" to the younger guys, and "Paper Lion" to the Kubiak generation.

With the bench, shuttle, and broad jump in the books, my group makes its way to the 40-yard dash, which has become the crown jewel of football talent evaluators. The players are upset because everybody is timing slow today. Chalk it up to the spongy turf and the fact that we're running alone, instead of being paired with another player to push each other down the field. The big linemen waddle through the 40 yards painfully, while players like Davis glide effortlessly through the yards, as if they were on ice skates. Watching the players run is a study in contrasts. There are the willowy-fast black guys whose cleats never seemed to touch turf. Perhaps my favorites are the short, squatty, strong fullback types who motor along low to the ground.

With the combine drills over, we move on to the business of playing football. Kubiak is clearly the most effective quarterback on the field during the seven-on-seven scrimmage, consistently getting the ball out on time and hitting receivers in stride.

"I feel good," said Kubiak, a phys ed teacher at Loy Norrix High School in Kalamazoo, Michigan. "Once I got out there and started going through things, the timing came back; it's just, at my age, you lose the zip and the explosion in your legs."

The pain in my ankle is something that I will feel good about the next day, but this day it just reminds me that I have a family to think about, and that football danger is real danger.

You walk it off. You try to look tough. You realize you are about to square off against a guy who was playing D-I ball last year, while in the mid-nineties you had a cup of coffee (more like a sip as a medical redshirt) at an NAIA school known more for theologians than gladiators, and then spent the last several years bouncing around the semipro leagues, trying to recapture the past. But it's all good. It's good to be breaking a huddle again. It's good to be lining up.

I catch Kubiak's eye as he walks off the field, grinning from ear to ear.

And that, I think, is the spirit of the thing.

I once interviewed a boxing manager who said that nervousness is the adult version of crying. If that's the case then right now I'm bawling my eyes out. Think Dick Vermeil watching *Beaches*.

In a matter of minutes I'll be hurling myself against real professional football players—guys who are bigger, faster, and stronger

than I am. They are milling around now in that time-honored tradition of looking tough and sizing each other up before a first practice. Sidelong glances are exchanged. T-shirts are read. Mental notes
are made. There are plenty of the usual shaven-head-and-goatee-
toughest-guy-at-the-bar-looking guys, plus one wide receiver who
brought a posse—two girls with video cameras—to film his exploits.
This guy immediately scores points in my book—I hope he makes
the team on that alone, but the fact of the matter is that whatever
the gimmick is, it's just a coping mechanism at this point because
everybody is on edge.

The plan for today is to go in helmets and shoulder pads, which
as everyone who has played any organized football (especially on a
first practice day) knows means full speed, full contact. The first
night of contact work has everybody a little jittery. These are grown
men, many of whom had already spent a tiring day at work, and are
now about to cross the threshold into a frightening place. Contact
work determines where you are physically, how you deal with fear,
and whether you still "have it." Personally, it has been three years
since I've had any contact on a football field, and I have spent a nervous week and an even more nervous drive to the facility (bathroom
stops: three) wondering if I still "have it." "It" being the balls to hit
another grown man, full speed.

At this point there are still nearly thirty players present who
won't be here when final cut-downs are made in a couple of weeks,
which means that everyone is trying to make a name by tattooing
someone else.

At twenty minutes before practice, I am worried for a number of
reasons, namely, that the intern (I never get a name, only, "The Intern") who is supposed to bring my gear hasn't shown up yet. I pass
the time talking to Brian Dolph, one of the two Battle Creek Crunch
players already signed to an actual contract. Dolph, I learned, played
at Saginaw Valley State where he broke numerous school records (I
didn't learn this from Dolph, who is a humble kid, rather, I looked it
up online) and played a couple of years in the AFL with the Indiana

Firebirds. Dolph is tall (think, Joe Jurevicius) with good hands and a friendly face who, interestingly, is one of the few players willing to make meaningful small talk—probably since he is also one of the few who doesn't have to prove himself today.

Finally, my equipment arrives and I spend a few awkward moments trying on helmets and shoulder pads while trying to dodge little soccer players racing around me on all sides, and their little fathers, racing closely behind.

The players have gathered on the field and I'm "taking a knee": leaning on my helmet, listening to the first-practice ritual of the coaches droning on about things such as Commitment and Hard Work. The huge lineman next to me explains that "taking a knee has got to be the worst thing about football." I agree that he has a point. You kneel down in your shorts, digging your naked knee into the rough, pebbly turf and try to sit there with a stern but interested look on your face while the coaches pontificate. I wonder why it is so important to take a knee? Perhaps it is so they can perpetually talk down to you. Coaches very rarely look you in the eye—they always want you sitting or kneeling.

There are considerably more black guys than white guys, and there are tattoos everywhere—from the uncreative (barbed-wire, tribal), to the incoherent (GODCHILD, written in huge letters across a stomach), to the reverent (an eight-inch portrait of the crucified Christ on the arm of a fat lineman), and everywhere in between. It seems like everybody has tattoos these days. I'm only twenty-nine, but an old twenty-nine. I've always wanted a tattoo, but the mantle of being a good, conservative, white boy has kept me from the parlor. I know that if I got one I would always regret it, but for some reason I want one anyway. A tattoo is not necessarily a representation of the depth of one's beliefs, however, because the lineman with the tattoo of Christ crucified on his arm is engaged in a detailed commentary on the talents of a stripper he met in Kalamazoo the night before.

Fast-forward thirty minutes. Dolph is loping downfield under spirals and I am about to square off with a 275-pound FB/LB from

Grand Rapids Community College named Antwuan Allen. I immediately regret my position choice and think about how intelligent George Plimpton was for choosing quarterback—leave it to a Harvard guy to know what he's doing. That said, I am still completely jacked on adrenaline—in other words, the physiological response that allows young people to do things they shouldn't do. We're working on a flow drill which means that there are two linebackers taking pursuit angles against one running back—in this case, the author. I have already fumbled once so my biggest priority is securing the football and turning upfield—there will be no moves made because these advanced maneuvers are better left to professionals. After taking the pitchout and charging upfield, I Fade to Black, as Metallica so eloquently wrote.

As quickly as I am crushed under the weight of Allen and Dewayne Thompson (veteran of the collegiate and semipro ranks, as well as a couple of CFL tryouts), I am up and walking along the boards, attempting to get my bearings. I feel a throb in my right hip and thigh, where Thompson's helmet intersected with my flesh. It hurts, and already I'm thinking about how bad it will hurt tomorrow. But it's important to try not to show how hurt you actually are— because everyone is looking, and most of them don't know I'm a writer moonlighting as a football player.

A note on collisions: whatever NFL players are making, they deserve it. This stuff really smarts. If you get a chance, stand on the field for a college or pro practice to get a feel for the noise generated by these hits. It's disconcerting. We're training at a suburban indoor soccer facility and drawing a lot of confused looks from platinum-blond soccer moms and floppy-haired kids in Umbros— like the hordes have descended to plunder their city.

Soon it is my turn again and I find myself at the front of the line: this time, in a variation of the drill, with a defensive lineman in front of me. It is up to me to read the movement of the running back and meet him in the "hole" vacated by the two linemen, who would push each other out of the way. I settle into the familiar linebacker's crouch—a position with knees bent just above ninety degrees and hands resting on knee pads. It is often called the "hit position" or the "football position" and is one from which the player can move quickly forward, backward, or to either side. On this play, however, I will only have time to make a decision and move forward in either direction. My adversary is an athletic-looking running back in a Detroit Seminoles helmet.

At the whistle, I bounce to the balls of my feet and lock eyes with the back. It is an intimate dance—in this case his eyes truly are a window into his intentions. For a moment all sound and life outside the blue dummies cease to exist as the ballcarrier, I, and our respective linemen move in unison. It is a meaningless drill in a life full of meaningless drills but today it feels as if everything is riding on my performance. I feel like I'm gliding as the back makes his move and I shuffle to the left of the collapsing linemen. An orange cone hems us in and now it is just the runner and me left to collide, with the only drama being who will get the better of the collision. I aim my helmet at a midpoint on his chest, trying my best to "blow him up." I miss, however, because he is far too good, but I end up sinking my shoulder into the exposed part of his belly between the breastplate and the belt line. We both exhale audibly and I continue driving my legs as we both hurtle turfward. We hit the ground and the world once again begins to exist. A whistle blows, we are pulled apart and the dance is repeated with different sets of players. I walk back to the end of the line with hands on hips and my head held high. I give the back a nod and he nods back. I know that tomorrow he will probably not remember the drill but it is one that I will more than likely remember for a long time. This time my body worked in concert with my brain and the job was done right.

After several more collisions in the linebacker drills I am fortunate to make the acquaintance of Crunch kicker Chuck Selinger, the other of the contracted players. Like all good kickers, Selinger has already figured out the angles—he knows how low his trajectory will have to be to clear the scoreboard at Kellogg Arena, how many points he'll get for drop-kicking a field goal (it's legal in this league and you get 4 points) and gives me the relative merits of FieldTurf versus the old Astroturf that we'll be playing on when games start. Selinger (a four-year starter at Central Michigan University) is a pharmaceutical sales rep by day, and he explains the nuances of the kicking game much like I would imagine he explains the advantages of the latest cure for hypertension or a swollen prostate. I appreciate his normalcy—he's one of the few players here who looks like he wasn't weaned on a steady diet of creatine and death metal—and after firing a few long snaps in his direction, the three-hour practice mercifully ends.

Postpractice my body is a bas-relief road map of pain. I am purple from shoulder to elbow and my arms sport an interesting array of little polka-dot welts (from the mesh practice jersey) and FieldTurf abrasions. There is a nice, purplish bruise around the outer portion of my right eye (thank you, Antwuan Allen) and if my wife harbored any excitement about sleeping with a professional athlete it is for naught—my plan is to not be touched by anyone for any reason, for several days. Sexy.

The bruises provide a sort of working diary of where I've been on the field. During the season, the right shoulder is a grotesque shade of purplish green, residue no doubt from the injury I sustained a couple of years ago. It flares up each year to varying degrees, but because the shoulder remains functional and just painful, I let it go, figuring it's much easier and more cost-effective to manage the pain on my own. Postpractice, I will generally peel off my pads, jersey, and pants; sit down on the cold porcelain toilet seat; and zone out while my wife goes to work dispensing peroxide and care into the various wounds. She will make much of me, rub my sore muscles, and generally reinforce the idea that she must have been sent directly from God Himself.

Later that night, at a group dinner with some friends, a college girl sums it up best. My various bruises, and the beating I took earlier in the evening, have provided fodder for a lively conversation. She's the kind of girl who probably plays volleyball and dates 6-foot-8 power forwards named Sven. She is interested in the book project, and wants to know where we'll be playing and what position I play. Running back and linebacker, I tell her.

"Really?" she says, incredulous. "You're so tiny."

After practice, I agree to meet in the mornings with Chuck Selinger, the kicker, to practice snapping (me) and kicking (him) at a golf dome in Jackson, Michigan. The first day there is a fresh snow falling, and I wind my way past the fast-food joints and industrial parks to find the dome. Selinger's minivan is idling in front of a locked gate.

"We're waiting for the guy that runs the embroidery shop in the back," he says. I open the door and hop into the van with Selinger—it is a mix between "mid-thirties father" and "working space." There is a laptop set up where he surfs league information. I quickly learn that Selinger already knows more about the league and our teammates than I do. He is a guy who prides himself on having and distributing information, which is a positive, since communication from the team is spotty at best. Selinger, who doesn't trust the team to actually outfit him with equipment, has set up his own meeting with the Adams USA equipment representative.

After several minutes of waiting, the embroidery guy, a soft-looking man of indiscriminate middle age, shows up and we are led into a cold, drafty golf dome. Cold and drafty, but pretty much the only space in mid-Michigan where we can practice kicking and snapping in the middle of January. Selinger goes through a regimented routine in which he kicks five balls at prescribed distances, getting longer as the workout progresses. He is kicking not at uprights but between ridges in the inflatable golf-dome walls. Selinger is chatty, which I appreciate. Most football player types are either trash talkers or stone silent upon first meeting. I learn that although he hasn't kicked competitively for nine years, he was a four-year starter at Central Michigan University and works summers as an instructor at a kicking camp there.

"I had a private tryout with the Grand Rapids Rampage set up six years ago," he says, "but the day before the workout they signed Remy Hamilton." Hamilton is a former University of Michigan star and one of the most respected kickers in the indoor game.

After Selinger kicks I have the opportunity to wrench on a cold helmet (it hurts), bend over the football, in pads, and fire my first significant batch of snaps in several years. The ball lasers back into Selinger's waiting hands as if on a rope. This feels good, it's like riding a bike, I think to myself. I am snapping in a pair of Under Armour gloves I purchased for the season. The gloves have a tackified, rubbery grip to them and, I feel, help me get a better grip on the ball when I'm snapping. It also doesn't hurt that they look extremely cool. I walk out to the car puffed up, feeling for the first time like a professional football player, and I like the feeling.

"Sorry I was late fellas," Embroidery Guy explains on the way out, "I had a tanning appointment." Selinger and I exchange sidelong glances. That's not really the kind of thing you admit publicly, in the company of men.

A phone call the day-of informs me that our second practice will be at an indoor golf dome in Schoolcraft, Michigan, which is even farther from my home than the soccer place in Kalamazoo. My body, the festering mass of bruises and soreness, seems to have improved a bit from the first practice, a feeling that lifts my spirits. My momentarily lifted spirits crash again, however, when I see the turf that we'll be practicing on tonight. It sucks. It is a hard, rough sheath of green pulled over concrete and drizzled with sand. I am reminded that this is a golf dome and the only feet that tread this turf are those of the poor sucker who has to go and retrieve the balls. In other words, this isn't a playing surface.

In other news, I think I have a concussion. The mysterious bruise on the side of my right eye, near my temple, is still there. I have experienced dizziness and general lightheadedness throughout the week, which is unusual for me; I rarely get so much as a headache. I tried to lift weights once during the week and got a little dizzy so I had to stop. Needless to say, this all has me a little worried. My brain, for better or worse, is my livelihood at this point. The horror stories about NFL players dealing with concussions—such as Merrill Hoge forgetting where he lived while driving home one day—and myriad players such as Troy Aikman, Chris Miller, and Steve Young, who have had multiple concussions, gives me pause. And these are only the high-profile guys, not the linebackers and fullbacks who lead with their heads every day.

There are some new bodies here tonight but there are some that have weeded themselves out already. The numbers are smaller than they were before, but already leaders are emerging. Carmell Dennis, the big linebacker who played at Oklahoma and Carson Newman, looks the part, and the thought of squaring off against him again tonight in the individual drills gives me a stomachache. He's the kind of guy who players will adjust their position in line in order to avoid. Chesaurae Rhodes and Darrell Johnson (two girls, one video camera—he's the guy), the receiving tandem from Detroit, are still projecting confidence; they have ascended the stairs of the dome to dress on the second level, away from the madding crowd. I climb the stairs to say hello. Rhodes is a friendly kid who always has a smile on his face and a word or two of encouragement to share. Tonight he compliments my gloves, the aforementioned sweet pair of black Under Armours, which, I assure him, I will try to do justice to with my play. Rhodes is one of the few guys who knows I'm a writer. He's seen the columns, he says, complimenting my work, which in addition to making me feel good does remind me that writing (not football) is my work.

Back downstairs Kenny Kubiak (age thirty-nine) reeks of Flexall but tells me that his body is feeling good. He's lying. I lie to him and tell him I'm feeling good, too. That's what athletes do, primarily, we lie to each other—at least until we find out who we can trust.

"We can't take people who don't know how to act," says Head Coach Bob Kubiak to the team, before practice. "The fans are very close and involved at this level. They let kids down on the field for autographs after the game. Whether or not you know how to act, at least fake it. This is professional football."

Nervous laughter.

There is a new kid here tonight, a new FB/LB in my group. He has a deranged, slightly retarded, look in his eyes. I recognize the look as a mix of unchecked nerves and testosterone. He is telling anyone who will listen about his boxing career, and about how he turned pro recently or something. I can tell by looking at him that he won't last through the first cut, not because of any perceived lack of talent, but just because he doesn't have the body type to play FB/LB at this level. As we jog through warm-ups I keep an eye on him, and end up squaring off with him in a half-speed "fit" drill in which the ballcarrier (me) jogs toward the line of scrimmage and the linebacker just gets into good-form tackling position, wraps his arms and lifts. The drill is supposed to be just a warm-up. A jog-through. A way to shake out some of the cobwebs from last week. But as I jog through the drill I realize that Retarded Boxer Kid is going full speed, eyes ablaze, just as he sends a right uppercut crashing into my nuts.

The next few minutes are kind of a blur. In the bathroom, after I make sure nothing is bleeding and everything (*ahem*) is working correctly, I take a moment to look in the mirror and reflect. Rather, I guess the moment takes me as I'm standing in front of the sink with a wet paper towel wiping blood off a fresh turf burn on my left elbow. It's weird to take this time to actually look at my face, something I rarely do in the morning when I'm just shaving or whatever. I notice a couple of gray hairs—I'm growing my hair out in a feeble attempt to look cool—and the beginnings of crow's-feet radiating out from my eyes. I see little droplets of my blood on the sink and realize that this is probably the first time this golf-dome sink has seen little droplets of blood. There is a quaint cross-stitch of a dumpy-looking fat golfer above the paper towel dispenser that says something about the nineteenth hole. I hear a pack of golfers laughing from the lobby. I suddenly wish I could hang out with them and laugh, too, but if I stay in here much longer somebody might think I'm soft. Soft is the kiss of death on a football team. So I leave and walk past the middle-agers blasting golf balls onto a computerized screen with a *thwack* of iron on ball followed by the hollow thud of ball hitting screen (it looks really fun—note to self: I really should try golf).

Back out on the field I aggravate an injury to the shoulder I separated a couple of years ago. It's the kind of pain that's manageable, but will keep me from lifting much weight for the rest of the season. As I pick myself up, I am reminded of how unforgiving the golf-dome turf can be. It's like landing on rough concrete. Out of the corner of my eye I notice a guy from my group, who wore "Cal Football" shorts and looked fairly athletic, packing up his gear. He looks upset, and I can tell that he is wasting no time in getting his stuff off and getting out of there. Perhaps he has realized that he is over-matched, or perhaps this is just no longer fun for him anymore. At any rate, he exits the dome's revolving door, never to be seen or heard from again.

I skip practice tonight which is a rarity for me—in fact, I've never really done it before.

"I don't feel bad about this," I explain to my wife. "It's no big deal—this is my hobby and not my life. No big thing."

The fact of the matter is that I'm guilt ridden and a horrible liar, and my wife knows it.

I'll spend the evening puttering around the lawn, taking a walk, taking care of an ant problem, and generally doing things that normal people do in the evening when they're not playing football.

As a younger man I had the devotion of a Baptist when it came to practice and workout attendance: if the doors were open, I was there. Now though, there is family, job obligations, a position on a nonprofit board, and the reality that two hours each night at practice doesn't hold the appeal that it once did. Even at practice, I find myself asking the coaches for the time. The truth is, I love being with my wife in the evening, and every minute spent somewhere else is a sacrifice.

Tonight we will read together and go to bed early—and by the end of the evening I will have forgotten about practice completely.

We recently watched the movie *About Schmidt*, starring Jack Nicholson and Kathy Bates, about a guy who gets to the end of a his life (after a successful career as an actuary for Woodmen of the World insurance company in Omaha) and realizes he hasn't done anything of worth. He has commuted to the same drab office, to do the same drab job, to buy nice things for the same drab suburban house, every day of his life. He has an estranged daughter and no significant friendships to speak of. Schmidt begins sponsoring a child from some godawful, impoverished African nation after seeing one of those Sally Struthers commercials about how "a cup of coffee a day" blah blah blah. He writes the child impassioned letters about his life and its lack of purpose, throughout the film.

The movie reminds me a great deal of my football experience in that, for the past several weeks I have been obsessed with the perfection of a field goal snap. Basically throwing the ball 7 yards between my legs, while looking backward at the kicker and the holder. That has been my life of late, which is a sad commentary. The ability to be obsessed with this is either a privilege, or a huge sign of mental unhealth. But I have stopped short of writing letters and sharing my feelings with third-world children. For now.

A dinner party with friends reveals other subtle road marks in my journey away from reality. My friends are going on and on about the cheese. The cheese, they say, a ten-year-old Wisconsin white cheddar procured at a hip, upscale city market (the kind of market designed by architects to look old), is fantastic. Ditto for a mango encrusted brie. What a pleasure. Don't we sound old, they say, all we talk about anymore is cheese. Ha ha. I sit at the end of the table, picking at a huge scab over my turf burn, bored out of my mind. If this is adulthood, if this is all there is, we're all in trouble.

"How's the Astroturf treating you?" my buddy asks. I can tell he wants to talk about it, so I tell the table a little bit about the project.

"Yeah, I talked to Joe the other day about what you're doing and he said that he wanted to play," he continues.

As if this is rec league where you can just show up and play. Joe needs a reality check. I wonder if he wants to live with turf burns, anxiety before every practice, and a chronically sore shoulder. Why this bothers me so much, I couldn't say. I like Joe.

"Well, I told him that when I worked out with you—and keep in mind you're a much bigger guy than I am"—the table nods in the affirmative, yes, I am a big guy, as I feel like a museum piece—"that you were blowing me away in the sprints."

This lifts my spirits, before he finishes with the hammer.

"But then I told him that you were like the smallest, slowest guy on your team."

"As-bury got a little black in him, look at his nose." Azriel Woodson, or "Aze" as he is known, is commenting on Crunch line coach Anthony Allsbury, who played collegiately at Western Michigan University, finishing in 2003. Like so many of my teammates, Allsbury is a pharmaceutical rep in the daytime, trekking from office to office, dropping off samples, and providing lunch for the doctors and nurses. His job is to be an impressive-looking, rapport-building, charming ex-athlete. Deliver the food. Get the Doc to sign his paper saying that he did indeed visit and did indeed drop off the Cialis samples. "Drug repping is glorified food service," according to a doctor friend of mine. Hence Allsbury's need for football, for a way to break the monotony of real life. As a player he was an

All-Mid-American Conference DE for two years running and a fringe NFL prospect, but a torn ACL and MCL in his senior year crushed the NFL dream.

As a coach he is still working out his identity but seems to be settling on the snarly, Jon Gruden thing. He stalks around practice in a backwards-turned New York Yankees hat, pulled low over his ears, and to a point where it sits just above his eyes so as to create the most intimidating effect. He doesn't yell so much as he barks at his players. His yelling is already becoming the object of parody and admiration among the ballplayers. "Laaackkksheiide . . . get your ass over here!" can be heard booming across the practice field at random times, and Allsbury often participates in the drills that he runs. Selinger and I have an unofficial bet as to when Allsbury will actually come out of retirement and suit up for us because he is clearly a man who hasn't yet reconciled himself to being an ex-player. My money is on Game 3, at Rochester, after the bye.

I am also pretty sure Allsbury can't stand me. He is the youngest of the coaches—younger than I am—and he is the only one who hasn't expressed interest or excitement in the project. He probably thinks it's preposterous for an "outsider" to infiltrate the intensely rarefied world of a football team, but then again he's right out of college where his football experience was regimented and predictable, whereas the other coaches—Ashe and Kubiak—have semipro football and its collection of characters in their background.

The black players like Allsbury because their unofficial anthropologic experiments (teasing, observation) have uncovered the mystery of his ethnic ambiguity—he is half black. The white players like him because we have no choice—if you don't buddy up to a coach like this (laugh at his jokes, and the like) he can make your life hell. These are the things you learn during training camp.

"Some of you guys need to watch what you eat," Allsbury tells a group of black players after practice one evening. "I know you guys like to eat fried chicken and everything . . ."

"Now that's a racial comment if I ever heard one," interrupts Coach Ashe.

"Hey, I'm half black," Allsbury replies.

After a minute of silence, L. J. Parker, a black linebacker from Indiana chimes in: "Does that mean I can kick half your ass then?"

As a team we are like a pack of diasporic tribesmen, waiting patiently for an announcement on the team Web site as to where and when our next practice will be because space for thirty-plus grown men to launch footballs and hit each other is at a premium. Our facilities range from the cookie-cutter suburban soccer complex to the slightly ghetto Triple Threat Sports Facility, which is basically a big aluminum pole barn with a handful of basketball courts stretched end to end.

It is here, at Triple Threat, that the majority of our training camp practices take place. I am learning the drive to Battle Creek from Lansing like the back of my hand. It takes almost an hour to the minute. An hour and five if I have to stop to get gas, which it seems as if I do every night. Take 496 West to 69 South to 94 West to 194 to Dickman Road to Twentieth Street South. Monday nights are my favorite because it is jazz night on 88.9 FM college radio. I have been on a search to find the music that most relaxes me before practice. I used to be a metal freak—Metallica, Pantera, Megadeth. A real maniac. In high school and college I would listen to this stuff and work myself into a violent froth before each practice and game. But I'm thirty, and I just can't do the metal anymore before practice. I'm nervous enough without music that pumps in extra intensity. I try the Christian channel once in a while, thinking the purity will do me some good, but it almost mellows me out too much. It makes me want to hug somebody and pray for them, or have a conversation about theology, which on its own is a good thing but kind of sucks before you're fixing to go out and jack somebody. So jazz it is. And it's real jazz, not the elevator-ready smooth-jazz variety. It's music that's got a bit of a swagger to it, that knows it's dangerous enough to make a difference. That's the kind of player I used to dream about being.

The tribe assembles at Triple Threat for another practice tonight. We wheel in our cars and I see scenes that I've seen a hundred times before at semipro practices. Large guys spilling out of their vehicles, carrying their shoulder pads slung over their helmets. The confident guys, or the guys with buddies, laugh and joke around while the rest of us just file in, stone faced, past the old-timers playing pickup basketball and the parents who look at us like we're two-headed freaks. Sometimes I look a court over and envy the old-timers and their casual hoops games. They have mastered the art of playing for the fun of it. They pick each other up when they fall down, they take frequent breaks, and look to just be high on the fact that they're still moving around, playing a real sport while most of their friends can't or don't. But then I feel my chinstrap, adjust my pads, and realize that this is the kind of sentimentality that will get me beat down. I have plenty of years to play pickup basketball, provided I get through this in one piece.

At Triple Threat we go up a set of rickety stairs to a landing that sits about 20 feet up above court level. It is here that team owner Mike Powell sets up shop on a folding table each night with his laptop computers and papers spread out in front of him. Sometimes the coaches will meet informally with Powell, but most nights he is there alone, going about the solitary business of being a minor league owner. He has the kind of face that shows worry. Like me, he is light-complected and slightly ruddy, and the worry is flushed onto his face almost nightly. I wonder sometimes if this is satisfying for him. Or if it is somehow less than what he expected.

I have pretty much kept to myself thus far, bantering once in a while with Ches (Chesaurae Rhodes) and Selinger when he appears at these practices. But I have decided tonight to be more proactive in approaching my teammates. I sidle up to Steve Brady, a tall, balding OL/DL prospect who played collegiately at Ball State University near where I grew up. I am curious about all of the players. What are their day jobs? How do the rigors of moonlighting as professional football players affect their jobs and their families?

"I'm a cop," explains Brady, to my surprise because he doesn't have what I stereotypically think to be the usual maladjusted cop attitude. "I work the night shift in a pretty rough part of Battle Creek. I work from 10 P.M. to 6 A.M. every night, which makes this pretty difficult."

Brady looks discouraged and tired, as do many of the guys, as the drive (players come from as far away as Detroit) and the late practices (usually from 8 to 10 P.M.) are wearing the players out.

Before drills we gather in a corner of the gym for individual pictures to be published in the team media guide and program. Because none of the players have seen so much as a Crunch T-shirt for our efforts thus far, we all share the same oversized Crunch pullover for the pictures. One guy gets his mug shot taken, peels off the pullover, and immediately gives it to the next guy. The pullover seems to be sized about XXXL and fits me like a large tent. The key, with football pictures, has always been to look as big and as mean as possible. Nobody smiles. Many do the upturned chin "want a piece of this?" big-neck pose. Most just stand there impassively, tight-lipped, producing a jailhouse mug-shot effect. Smiling, of course, would imply that one is soft. The only other guy, besides me, that smiles is 6-foot-3, 230-pound linebacker, L. J. Parker, and everybody knows he's not soft.

It is practice as usual as we gather in the middle of the floor, spaced in lines 5 yards apart, for calisthenics. Some of the players take the stretching seriously, while others use it as a time to relax and goof off. After stretches, we do a series of warm-up runs such as high-knees, carioca (a dancelike maneuver in which we cross our feet going sideways), shuffles, and finally half-speed sprints. After a breakdown—teams always "break down" at various points throughout the practice, yelling things like "Championship!" or "Hard work!" or if feeling uncreative, just "Crunch!"—we move to our respective position groups.

The fullbacks/linebackers always gather in a corner of the gym with Coach Scott Ashe. As a coach, Ashe is probably the most self-assured of the three. He is a Michigan semipro legend, having played and coached for the Jackson Bombers and Downriver Raiders, teams that both won national titles. He also had a short coaching stint with the Detroit Drive in the Arena Football League that gives him instant credibility here. Ashe is intense, but his intensity is less contrived, as opposed to Allsbury's showmanship. They all, however, have "coach walk" (limping, as a result of years in the game) and "coach talk" (a couple of octaves lower than necessary) as a part of their repertoires.

Ashe has already offered a one-hundred-dollar bounty on the head of Port Huron quarterback Shane Franzer for our first game. And his favorite motto is, "When in doubt, knock him out." Ashe is coaching the linebackers now, imploring us to hit wide receivers within the 5-yard "box" as they drift across the middle. "If he comes across the middle," Ashe says, "knock his dick-string loose." I bite my lip to keep from laughing. Ashe knows this stuff is funny, which is half the reason why he says it.

After running through our drills, we join the wide receivers in their passing lines, running short curls, slants, and go routes. This is basic football, the kinds of things we've been doing on practice fields and in backyards our entire lives. I am catching the balls—my hands have always been decent—but without the flair and panache of the wide receivers, perhaps the most intentionally stylish position in football. Many of the guys, especially the guys that have played professionally before, will cradle the football in with one hand. The receivers are the most put-together, even in their practice attire. Except for one guy, Donnie Lonsway, who doesn't look the part of a professional athlete. Lonsway has a scruffy beard, an old helmet, and wears rib pads to practice each day—quite a departure from the studied hip-hop culture of the typical wide receiver.

"I'm thirty-two and I've been playing football for as long as I can remember," he says after practice. "I love it. You put on the helmet and you feel like you're putting on a suit of armor. We're like modern-day gladiators. It always feels good, too, as a receiver, when you take a big hit and can pop right back up."

I ask Lonsway how he met Coach Kubiak, and how he became involved here.

"The short answer is that I just found out about the tryouts and showed up," he says. "But I played football for three years at Olivet College when Kubiak was the offensive coordinator there. After that I got a call from Bob, who at that time was with the Jackson Bombers, and he said 'I need a receiver'. I went and suited up that day and caught a pass for a first down on a fourth and twelve. I guess you could say I was hooked. The next year I had twenty-four touchdowns."

Lonsway went on to play at the semipro level throughout the 1990s, garnering semipro All-American honors for teams including the Bombers, Detroit Seminoles, and Kalamazoo Tornadoes. He manages a gas station in Kalamazoo during the day.

"I've never had anybody really stop me at any level," he says, not bragging. "I've probably caught at least 80 percent of the balls thrown to me throughout my career." He is silent for a moment. "I really don't know where I'd be without football," he says finally.

"How so?" I ask. Usually this is a statement reserved for athletes who have clawed their way out of the ghetto and are now enjoying the fruits of an NFL contract.

"I don't know how much detail you want," he says, apprehensive.

"As much as you're comfortable with," I reply.

"When I was about twelve, I was so sick of life. My dad and I had an abusive relationship . . . I had a shotgun in my room and I thought about it a lot, you know. But I finally left and said 'I've gotta go to practice'. So in a way, football saved my life."

I ask about his father now, and if he has been able to share any of his football successes with him.

"I've seen him at some of my semipro games," he says. "He won't say anything to me but he'll just go up in the stands. Whenever I see him there I just leave immediately. I'll make sure the game is in hand but I'll leave—sometimes before the game is even over."

Chapter Four

The Past (or, Where I Live)

Where I grew up, a small (three stoplights, four convenience stores, six video stores) town in Indiana called Hartford City, excelling in athletics was one's only means of scaling the social ladder. It was the kind of place where "being somebody" meant getting your picture in the *News-Times* and having the old guys talk about you when they sat around getting their hair cut at Mitchell's Barber Shop. It was small-town idyllic in a Norman Rockwell sort of way, the kind of town you desperately want to leave at age seventeen, but that by thirty you want to go back to, if only to see a place where nothing changes. It's not the kind of town where parents "empty-nest" into huge houses in the suburbs. When I visit my friends I get to see their parents' homes as they were when I was a kid, and sit in the living rooms where we played. I've traveled the world, but for me, now, this is very important. It's important to know that sometimes people stay put.

When I was nine, I first tasted the fruit of adult praise, launching my helmet (containing my head) into another child carrying a football. The sharp crack of plastic on plastic resonated across the field causing the fathers—insurance agents, factory workers, schoolteachers—to leave their seats and scream like savages. The joy rushed through my young veins like a drug and in the mind of a nine-year-old solidified the fact that I wanted to be a ballplayer. Approval is addictive that way.

"Run the fake dive, bootleg right," said my dad, a million times. The fake dive bootleg right required the fullback to plunge through the line, pretend to take a handoff, and then curl out into the flat to receive a pass from the rolling quarterback. It was a play that required timing and precision to work correctly.

I was nine and this was an evening spent like many others before and after it. Weather permitting, we would grab an official NFL Wilson football—quote former Lions' journeyman QB Carl Sweetan in *Paper Lion*: "There's something about a pro ball, it's got a certain feel about it"—and head to the largest available open plot of grass. When I was very young, the backyard was enough. As I grew older, however, it became a vacant lot, and finally the high school practice field. Once there, my father would call the routes and I would run them—route after route, night after night in the heat, the cold, and everything in between. Hooks, crossing routes, bootlegs, deep-out patterns, and go's—the smell of football would become permanently embedded in our fingers, and soon the routes would get easier, the throws more accurate. We would often try to re-create legendary plays such as Dwight Clark's "The Catch" and Franco's "Immaculate Reception"—running the plays to perfection. Sometimes the neighbor kids would join in, but not often, because they somehow knew these were work sessions. At the end I was exhausted. Too exhausted to rebel, and I had nothing to rebel against. My dad was spending his free time with me, and all was right with the world.

I would play much of my best football on those nights, and in the dark periods, in college after the injury, I would wonder if it was all a waste of time—all the work, that is. I would come to the realization later in life, however, that those nights were football, too—football just as much as Friday nights and Saturday afternoons under the lights. I would grow up and the neighborhood would grow up with me, eventually filling up all of the green, open spaces with houses, gardens, swingsets, and new people.

But it might have been the most important football I ever played.

I am actually a third-generation minor league ballplayer. My grandfather, or Gramps, or Turk, as he is known to whoever happens to be telling the story—the family's most promising athlete—was a running back for South Chicago's Clearing Ramblers, and a pitcher in the Cubs farm system. He was recruited by BorgWarner to play baseball for their company club. Having no interest in the tool-and-die industry but wanting to play ball, he signed on. In certain pockets of Chicago neighborhoods, and among certain men now in their late eighties, he was something of a legend. A blown shoulder sustained on a nameless football field against nameless competition would effectively end his future with the Cubs and send him into a career in the tool-and-die industry, in which he would become very successful. I knew, however, that nobody spun tales about tool-and-die men, and that when I went to visit, I wanted to see the pictures of Gramps in the leather helmet and pads. Those pictures now line my office—not because he was a sports hero—but because he was kind and took the time to have breakfast with me, early in the morning, which is where I learned to drink coffee and smoke a cigarette, among other things.

Semipro ballplayers toiled in obscurity for the ensuing decades until the NFL seemed to take notice in the fifties and sixties. It was then that semiorganized "farm systems" were set up in which NFL clubs would partially underwrite (some with money, uniforms, and players) the operating costs of semipro franchises in blue-collar cities such as Pottstown, Bridgeport, Joliet, Harrisburg, Racine, and Cheboygan. Finally, semipro clubs would have the capital needed to put a legitimate product on the field, and in many places, fans responded. They would pay a few bucks, fill up a local civic or high school stadium, and see good players playing generally decent football. Some of the players—most of them nameless and faceless—would put off the transition to "real life" for a few years in these bush leagues before going on to unremarkable careers in the NFL or Canada, which is no small accomplishment. Some diamonds, however—such as Otis Sistrunk and Johnny Unitas—were discovered in this rough. And in the meantime, they were able to hone their craft in friendly cities where they were treated like minor celebrities.

My dad, a center for Madison Mustangs of the Central States Football League, remembers: "We had several guys on our roster who had played in the Big Ten, and most of the guys were good, solid college players. The teams would recruit us out of college and each club had a guy in the "front office"—usually a local fan or businessman—who would go about getting each player that signed a day job in the community to put food on the table. I sold cars. And then the team would kick in a few hundred bucks a game. It was a good deal and something fun to do after college. And it was really good football. We got pretty decent coverage in the paper, too—it was a legitimate thing to do in Madison on a Saturday night. You had Friday night high school ball, Saturday afternoon you had the Badgers, Saturday night the Mustangs, and Sunday the Packers. It was a good area for football."

I remember flipping through Dad's old, glossy Mustang football programs as a kid. It seemed like a great way to live—a decent day job and then money to play on Saturday night.

A few years later, someone in the "league office" would steal money from the CSFL, and the league would fold. An ending not even dramatic enough to be called tragic. The players would find somewhere else to play. Or they wouldn't. Life would go on as life has a tendency to do.

In high school, the coaches told us to not "get caught up in all of that hoopla." But it was a small town and homecoming was probably the only hoopla most of these guys would ever experience. They were staring down the barrel of fifty years of unfulfilling work and I thought that if someone wants to throw you a bonfire and a parade and make much of you, you should take it and be thankful. But coaches, I found, often saw things through a different lens.

"You guys aren't going to have college careers, so this is the last game you're going to play," said Richardson, my high school coach. It was the night before homecoming and Richardson was trying, in his own, different way, to motivate us. He was trying to get us to realize how special it was to play there on Friday nights. To be, in essence, the only show in town.

Richardson was a short, barrel-chested man with a wild shock of white hair and spit perpetually flying out of his mouth. Perhaps his most notable characteristic as a coach was the fact that he was blessed with a deep, booming voice that would echo off the red-and-black lockers in the Blackford High School cleat house. He was one of those small-town fixtures—guys who stalk the sidelines for a million years, coaching every able-bodied male who grows up in the school system. He had coached the Blackford Bruins to a state championship in 1979, back when the veer option was still in vogue, and when Blackford was blessed with a stable of big, nasty farm boys who could run and hit. By the early nineties, when I was there, Blackford was still running a version of the veer option, which by then everyone knew how to stop, and Coach was still telling stories about the late seventies, because by the early 90's the big, nasty farm boys had turned into, with the exception of a few, a lot of apathetic 170 pounders. Still, I had a soft place in my heart for him. Richardson called me "Klucker" with warmth, mussed up my hair, and was one of the first to show up in the hospital when I broke my leg. We forged something resembling a relationship because I would often be the lone player to show up for summer workouts and we would spend an hour or two together in the hot weight room or out on the field. Richardson taught my senior-year sociology class, and he was talented and passionate in front of a classroom—unique for a coach. The fire that seemed so angry on the field somehow channeled itself in outstanding and creative ways as a teacher. To this day, when I go home to Hartford City, I still look for Coach's truck, the Valdez Cruiser, hoping to see him at the grocery store or the gas station. Not that I would know what to say to him—I'd probably stare very intently at the cereal or the gas pump and pretend I didn't see him at all. But I still cried like a baby and hugged him after my last high school game—a fact for which I am more than a little embarrassed, quite honestly. There's something about pleasing one's high school coach that really never goes away.

One day it worked perfectly. Athletics I think is a process of surviving all of the hard stuff—being cussed out by coaches, summer workouts, two-a-days, and the rest of it—and living for the moment when it all comes together. Every athlete has that day, be it in Pop Warner, high school, college, or even the professional level, when the stars seem to align and everything just kind of works out. For me, that day came in my junior year of high school.

I weighed about 205 pounds and was a starter at outside line-backer and offensive guard, believe it or not. We were a fairly small team, and if a guy was healthy and could play a little, he usually found himself playing the entire game. This particular game took place in the Hoosier (now RCA) Dome just a few years before Corporate America sunk its claws into stadium naming and gave us places such as Adelphia Coliseum, Enron Field, and 3Com Park. Charming.

It was our conference's "Dome Day," meaning that the conference would run games the entire day and we would be playing in front of the parents, farmers, drunks, and hair spray teased high school girls belonging to every school in our conference. They came from places like Tipton, Fairmount (birthplace of James Dean), and Elwood, Indiana, and it truly was heady stuff for a sixteen-year-old. Our first time on Astroturf to boot. Of course, in the grand scheme of things, none of it mattered much—it never really does—but for a day, that day, we were the feature presentation. We were heavy underdogs, but it was imperative that we won, because a loss would mean an hour-and-a-half bus ride home in silence.

Football Commandments indicate that the losing team must treat every loss as though it were the end of the world. Thou shalt ride the bus home in a shocked state of mournful silence—no doubt replaying the game in our little teenaged minds and trying to fix what went wrong. The coaches would sit stone-faced—in their Blackford High School Windbreakers—angrily chomping gum and offering up the occasional "Shut up back there," or "There's nothing funny about losing to Tipton" if there was a player brave enough to break the heavy silence with a story. Smiling or enjoying the fact that you were young and had just played a difficult game well made no difference—in the mind of a coach, losing was akin to death and was a pill to be taken quietly.

Our opponent, the Alexandria Tigers, boasted an All-State running back named John Eden who, rumor had it, was headed to Penn State on a football scholarship. This, in principle, made me want to take his head off because I loathed the idea that anyone besides me was going anywhere on a football scholarship. Secretly though, I wondered if I would be able to contain him—because it was my job to seal off the outside on tosses and sweeps. All week in practice, our coaches, when not imparting sage advice, such as "Try harder" and "Don't be soft," had implored me to seal off the outside at any cost. Except of course, giving up the inside run which I was not allowed to do either. If I could do both at the same time, however, my name would be Superman and all of this would be moot.

Per usual procedure, I nearly hyperventilated and vomited all over myself in the locker room before the game. It was a plush, spacious room that normally housed the NFL's Indianapolis Colts. Blue carpet. Blue chairs. Blue stalls. The bathrooms and showers actually had soap and aftershave, which none of us really needed but was nonetheless very cool.

Surprisingly, our team went out and put on a clinic. We were quite nearly unstoppable and nobody was more shocked than we were. Our antiquated playbook was actually working for us. And in the third quarter, my own momentary brush with nirvana happened when Alexandria ran a toss sweep to my side. Eden took the pitchout and I met him and brought him to the carpet in the backfield—a play that is undoubtedly nary a blip on the radar screen of his memory. He probably rarely thinks of the game at all. Following the tackle, I got up and struck an almost crucifix-like pose where I spread my arms and gazed heavenward toward about 45,000 empty seats—a pose that was forever frozen in time by our town's only reporter (my dad affectionately dubbed him "Jimmy Olsen") who ran the picture on the front page of the next day's paper. I think we bought about twelve copies.

Thank you, John Eden.

★ ★ ★

It was a cold, windy Indiana winter day that Dad and I drove down to Indiana University on a recruiting visit and I experienced what may have been my proudest few hours as a son. Indiana made it clear that they would have no scholarship money available but invited us in for a meeting. To a seventeen-year-old, visiting an NCAA Division I program is akin to visiting Mecca. I would be something called a "preferred walk-on," which is, I guess, somehow better than a regular walk-on.

I wasn't a great high school player. I had the broken leg, and was what is known in football circles as an "overachiever"—which, if your glass is half full means that you are an endearing, hustling, coach's dream. Whereas if your glass is half empty it means that you are a few inches too short, a few pounds too light, and a few steps too slow, and your career may very well be a study in frustration. That day, though, my glass was half full.

Indiana, thinking back, was probably more interested in the work ethic—in the fact that I had built myself into a decent-sized white tank through weights, and could press huge amounts of iron up from my chest—a talent that matters less the older one gets. They showed me around the football complex and I got my first taste of extravagance. They showed off the rows and rows of gleaming red helmets with the cream colored *I*. They showed me the boxes upon boxes of brand new turf shoes and gloves that are distributed to each player—shoes for wet turf, dry turf, short grass, long grass, and everything in between. I saw the spacious, carpeted locker room, and the whirlpool where a couple of current players soaked away their soreness. I remember thinking that for Division I stars they didn't look very happy. I was led into a plush theater, loaded down with glossy media guides, and shown *The Highlight Film*—it was like a one-man Hollywood premiere. Later, they would walk us through the cafeteria where the athletes ate specially prepared food, far from the madding crowd of the "traditional" university student. Finally, I was led outside and into the big, empty, 50,000-seat bowl for a moment that would be cheapened forever by recruiting scenes in movies such as *The Program*. They really do show you the stadium and it really is cool. And at seventeen you are dumbstruck and defenseless. It was a decidedly prethought age for me. I hadn't yet realized that there were chemistry labs and class buildings crumbling on campus while funding was pushed into already-rich athletic programs. It didn't yet register that barely literate athletes were herded into these universities like meat and left four years later without a degree and without their four acres and a mule. I, like most fawning fans, was blissfully oblivious.

I sat next to a college kid at a wedding reception once—a kid who played at Taylor University (an NAIA school) a few years after me and who I knew only as an acquaintance. The people at the table were all very impressed with this kid, having played four years of college ball and all.

"How did you stay healthy?" someone asked.

"I just worked out and prayed a lot," the kid responded.

A real pious guy. What a piece of work, this kid. There may not be anything in the world I hate more than piety, although I've undoubtedly been guilty of it myself.

"Didn't you play college ball?" someone else asked in my direction. I felt like I was in *The Graduate*. Wow, sometimes it sucked to be young.

"For a little bit, then I got hurt in my sophomore year. Broken leg. Must not have prayed hard enough."

Nobody got the sarcasm. I have a theory that everybody gets dumber at wedding receptions and this proved it.

"Let's get out of here now," I smiled and whispered in Kristin's ear. For all they knew, I was whispering sweet-nothings or asking if she wanted another drink.

The sad part is, she understood exactly why I wanted to leave.

My college career effectively ended in 1995 when I stopped eating during training camp of my sophomore year. It was hot that year, over a hundred degrees for several days straight, and the team was bunking in one of the oldest halls on campus, called Sammy Morris, named after a missionary. It was an old, roach-infested bunker that they would rebuild a few years later.

My roommate never reported to camp so I stayed by myself. Me, the cockroaches, a bottle of weight gainer, a radio, and a fan. It was one of those sweaty, melodramatic, "rock bottom" scenes that people have in the movies when they realize they need to change their lives. It was hard to sleep because I was obsessing about my performance in the previous day's practice and at the same time worried about what the next morning would hold. Would the temperature break? Would we be in pads? Will the surgically repaired leg ever stop throbbing? Would they make us weigh in, and would I lose eight pounds again? Then I would drift away into a hot sleep oven for a couple of minutes until the coaches blasted their air horns through the hall as a way to wake us up . . . assuming that we weren't smart enough to set an alarm clock and that we needed to be treated like cattle.

I had gone from a reporting weight of 247 to about 225 in a couple of days. It was hot and I was sweating like a madman before, during, and after practice. With every drop I worried that they would take away my scholarship and my identity when they discovered that what good is a 225-pound defensive end at the college level? Yet I couldn't bring myself to eat in the dining hall between practices. The thought of food made me want to vomit but I knew I was wasting away in football terms—even though I remained bigger, faster, and stronger than 90 percent of the general public. In football terms I was Ghandi on a hunger strike, which is pretty impractical for a college player.

In layman's terms, I was getting beat up, which I was not used to. I had always either dominated or at least been competitive before, but now, my leg wasn't working much at all and I couldn't move. If you can't move, you can't play, as the saying goes. I was devastated and my mind wasn't sure what to do with this newfound failure. I walked like a zombie from practices to meetings to meals to practices to meetings to sleep . . . used to being the king of the castle, I was burning in ego hell.

So one morning after breakfast I walked up to the head coach's office in the gymnasium and quit the team. I said something about the leg and it not being fun anymore and it being like a job. The coach, being the nice guy that he is offered to let me film or wash jocks or something to keep my scholarship. And being the short-sighted nineteen-year-old that I was, I said that I would rather die than be involved and not be a player. I probably got a little misty-eyed but remembered being able to keep it under control, which was nice for a change.

I left the office to find another hot summer day. The sun was shining and the sky hadn't fallen down. Some old friend of my parents who worked at the college gave me a thumbs-up and said "Go get 'em" or something equally lame, thinking I was still going to be busting heads on Saturday afternoons. I waved at him weakly. I was free of it all now. I felt equal parts devastated and elated. I packed up the tan pickup and drove home to begin the rest of my life.

Chapter Five

One More Summer in the Sun

For the first time in his thirty-six-year life, Carmell Dennis is a professional football player. He has played for, in no particular order, the University of Oklahoma, Central State University in Ohio, Hillsdale College (famous only for blue Astroturf and its Libertarian political bent), the United States military (in Iraq, not play), and Carson-Newman University. He looks the part. He stands about 6 feet, 3 inches and weighs 245. Prototype. His biceps are prototype. He has a sinister black visor on his helmet that is also prototype. Carmell Dennis also hits like a truck, as I found out the hard way at our first padded practice.

The Garfield Lake Tavern, on the outskirts of Olivet, Michigan (a town that is, in itself, an outskirt), resembles Bob's Country Bunker in the 1980 film *The Blues Brothers*. It's the sort of place where they have both kinds of music, country and western, and we, as a team, have gathered here after a preseason practice on the promise of ten free pitchers of beer as provided by team owner Mike Powell. The bar features absolutely no lights in the parking lot and has the distinction of not being near anything at all. I already fear for my ability to find my tiny, (ironically) midnight-blue Toyota Echo after the last of the sun dips under the horizon. Dennis, however, fears something else.

"Man, we took a wrong turn down a dirt road and I thought they was gonna lynch us coming up in here," he said, over a plastic cup of beer that seems positively engulfed by his large hands. "The hills have eyes in places like this!" Dennis is the kind of guy that is a leader on any team he is a part of, due in no small part to a menacing physique but also to a relatively friendly face and gift for banter.

He is filling me in on the nomadic journey that has been his football career up to this point.

"Man, I had to get out of Oklahoma," he says with a laugh. "They were shooting holes in the dormitories down there!"

This was a late eighties, just post–Bosworth, Oklahoma, that still featured legendary outlaw Barry Switzer as head coach. The team's reputation for chaos was a large as its reputation for winning football.

"I was there with Keith Jackson and a bunch of other guys who played in the league . . . I have friends in the league," Dennis adds. Dennis had his own brief tryout with the Oakland Raiders, after his final collegiate stop at Carson Newman. His stay was brief because the team decided to keep LB Sam Sword, ironically a high-profile University of Michigan product, over Dennis.

"I didn't even get to meet Al Davis," he adds. "If you weren't getting a contract, he didn't have nothing to do with you."

We are visited by several other Crunch players who have filed in and bellied up to the bar. The surroundings are Midwestern spartan—a few beer signs, pool tables, and lots of wood. It was purported to be (by 300-pound Crunch center and recent Olivet College grad Kyle Lacksheide) "ladies night" at the bar, however, apart from a couple of old guys in John Deere hats, and a few slumming frat boys in the corner, we are it. Someone asks Lacksheide if this is the only bar in Olivet. "The only one worth going to," he replies. Lacksheide, I learn, also bounces here once in a while.

The stories begin, and I learn that the players are all, to a man, remarkably down to earth. Many are over thirty and many are parents. I exchange potty-training stories with Tom Mack, a tall defensive end who sports a shaven head, goatee, and a variety of tattoos. Mack is a football junkie who also made short stops at several Michigan institutions of higher education, and a rabid University of Miami fan who buys season tickets (at the student rate) solely for the privilege of flying down each fall for the Miami versus Florida State matchup.

We are joined by massive offensive tackle Chris Gillette, who played collegiately at Toledo in the Mid-American Conference, and who has made the Michigan semipro rounds as well. Gillette is remarkably polished for an offensive lineman, and is always among the most put-together and respectable looking of the Crunch players. Shirt tucked in. Neat pullover sweater. Dark hair manicured. He ran the 40-yard dash (football's litmus test for speed and athleticism) in a very fast 5.1 seconds at 295 pounds. He also led the team with 32 reps of 225 pounds on the bench. He has been the object of some scorn today because, at the last practice, he rolled his ankle and screamed "It's broken! It's broken!" as he lay on the turf. "I was screaming like a French whore," he admits without a hint of shame. Gillette is, by day, a confectioner, working over a stove to produce small chocolate creations that he sells to area coffee shops. It seems an odd occupation for someone who is so large, and involved in such violent pursuits.

"I owned a semipro team for a year, the Battle Creek Rattlers," says Gillette. I ask him, surprised, what he thought of the experience.

"It was awful," he says without hesitation. "I'm a bad manager, that way." He goes on to describe, in some detail, player splits, and fund-raisers in which he was the only attendee, drinking himself into oblivion at the end of the night. Gillette's team endured a massive rift, in which half of his team defected to create another team in midseason. In spite of this, they still won four games.

"Every day, I regret the fact that I left Toledo with a year of eligibility remaining," he explains. "This season, with the Crunch, is all about making up for that last year."

I ask him, a father of two, how his wife felt about this latest comeback.

"I think she was glad it wasn't semipro," he says. "The last year I suggested playing semipro she pulled out the divorce papers and said, 'It's me or football'. I guess you could call that an ultimatum."

Defensive Coordinator Scott Ashe, himself a veteran of semipro wars as both a player and an owner, enters the bar. He cuts an impressive figure, standing about 6-foot-4 and boasting perhaps the most profane football vocabulary I've ever heard. If I had a nickel for every time coach Ashe used the phrase, "Let's hit these f—kers in the mouth," I would be a rich man. But Ashe is a good guy, I think. As he approaches Gillette, he looks to make sure he has an audience before shouting in a high-pitched voice: "It's broken! It's broken!" The place cracks up.

Crunch linebacker Azriel Woodson, a professional indoor veteran who last played in the United Indoor Football League with the Tennessee Valley Raptors, approaches as Dennis is sharing stories from his life in football. He has a cell phone attached to his ear, and shoots me a sidelong glance. Woodson, thus far, has been among the most standoffish of my teammates. I know he has read the articles because he has made reference to them on occasion, but has always seemed reluctant to talk. He is always quick with a scathing putdown, in that reasonably good-natured athlete sort of way. In spite of this I still find him intimidating. Dennis waves him over and he approaches, hesitantly, looking at me.

"He wearing the wire?"

He asks me if I fear for my life.

Ben is a classically trained pianist, a family man. Father of two beautiful children. Working on a degree in theology. I am telling him, for the first time, about my idea for this book. To train with and play football games as a member of the professional indoor Battle Creek Crunch of the Great Lakes Indoor Football League. He's trying to get a feel for where I fit in the big picture of things. He knew I played, a while ago, and that I was decent but not great, which is what I told everybody. I believed it. The beautiful thing about sports is that as athletes we all go through the different stages of development—we are participants as children, completely unselfconscious. And then, later, we become workmen, working toward a spot on the high school team, then later a college scholarship, and for the truly gifted, a professional career. And then, finally, someone tells us we're not good anymore and we become spectators. This happens to every athlete at every level of organized sport.

"So how good are you?" he asks.

"I'm not embarrassing myself," I reply. "But I'm getting the crap kicked out of me." It was nothing if not honest. Not a turn of phrase spoken by the typical concert pianist but a reasonable assessment of my first three weeks of contact work as a member of the Battle Creek Crunch. The players are good, I tell him, most played major college ball and were a twisted ankle or a tenth of a second away from the big time, the NFL.

"So do you fear for your life?" he asks. Our children are running around together, completely unaware of the conversation. I look at them and reflect in what I hope is a not-too-dramatic way on how beautiful they are.

"Yes," I reply. "Often."

Like most football players, I've been in and out of hospitals along the way, joking that they would name an emergency room after me at the Blackford County Hospital after an unfortunate string of high school injuries. As a senior in high school, I heard the leg snap in two during a routine tackling drill. I was carrying the football during a mid-September practice and some sophomore kid, I think his name was Jake or Jack or something, wrapped himself around my fibula and fell hard—breaking it in half. I immediately tried to stand up and "walk it off"—the time-tested football remedy— but denial only goes so far when you have heard your own leg break. I laid back on the grass and waited for this nice kid named Steve who owned an El Camino and was a pseudo player/trainer/manager to haul me back up to the cleat house where I at least hoped I would get the cute manager to put the ice on my leg. Ordinarily, a ride in the back of an El Camino would have been extremely cool, but under the circumstances it lost a bit of its luster.

An assistant coach, a young guy named Shane Robbins, drove me to the hospital, where I waited for about two hours with my shattered leg and dreams propped up on a waiting room coffee table.

Robbins undoubtedly said cool things about how the leg would heal quickly and it wouldn't effect my college career adversely. The leg throbbed horribly though, and the kindly 300-pound nurses wouldn't relinquish anything stronger than Advil to dull the pain. There was a marathon of Batman cartoons playing on the waiting room television and I thought it a strange juxtaposition—the mirth of a cartoon coupled with life as I liked it being over.

Hartford City is a town that extends about two miles in each direction, making it all the more unfathomable that it took two hours for a doctor to make it into the emergency room. My dad, meanwhile, made the sixty-mile trip from Fort Wayne in a little under an hour. Finally, the doctor appeared and I was given the privilege of removing my football pants and lying in a hospital bed. It's funny, in an ironic sort of way, to hear bad news while not wearing any pants—but when you're an injured athlete this is often the case.

Someone comes in and tells you what is happening to you physically while your nakedness hangs out the back end of a too-small gown, adding to the paranoia that comes from doctors basically having dominion over your body. The doctor didn't bother to set the leg and simply slapped an air cast on it, told me my season was over, wrote a prescription for some anti-inflammatory stuff, and took off. I figured he probably had a golf game to get to or something—hence the rush. A note about doctors: Ever notice how they seem to enjoy telling you that your season is over? Especially the doctors who are particularly short, fat, old, or unathletic. You know, the ones who could never in a million years play a sport (golf notwithstanding) themselves.

Before I would hobble home and learn to walk on crutches, Coach stopped by and said something kind and appropriate. I wept and immediately felt sheepish about it.

If you want to go for the glory you have to deal with this. Those were her words not mine. And "this," was a sleepless night made sleepless because of one bad snap that bounced back toward the holder (Donny Lonsway) instead of spiraling back in a neat laser-like motion that brings a great deal of satisfaction to only the long snapper and maybe the holder and kicker. Snapping is a crap job. A raw deal. The worst job in sports. I dribbled the snap back and immediately the coaches started yelling for anyone else who could long snap. I felt very much like a writer in that moment. I might as well have been wearing a pair of khakis and a golf shirt, as out of place as I felt. As if sensing my pain, Ashe explained that "if that happens in a game we'll cut your balls off." Nice.

The team has endured another round of cuts and some familiar faces are gone. One of my favorite players, Eric Vandenberg, a special-ed teacher and family man, is noticeably absent. "I'm working four jobs," he told me in a previous practice. "Roofing, teaching, fixing up a house to sell . . . and this, if you count this as a job." Vandenberg was a gritty safety (honorable mention All-Conference at Grand Valley State as a senior) who really had no position in the indoor game. He didn't have the bowling-ball type fullback body to play in the offensive backfield, nor was he quite fast enough to survive in man-to-man coverage. A classier guy it would be hard to find, however. In an attempt to spend more time with his family he dutifully brought his wife and toddler to each practice. He will make more of an impact in his classroom that he would whiling away his hours on a twelve-hour bus ride to Rochester. Maybe he's the lucky one.

As we plod off the practice field Ken Kubiak is not feeling lucky. He has recently learned that his younger (relatively speaking) brother, Tim (age thirty-two), will get the nod as starting quarterback in Friday's opener versus Port Huron.

"I was pretty pissed," he explains. Kubiak looked extremely sharp today in practice. He is a physical educator at Loy Norrix High School in Kalamazoo, his brother a middle school math teacher. "I didn't like the way it was handled, primarily . . . I thought he let me know in an unprofessional way," he continues.

This would be perfectly normal and that much less awkward if his brother, Bob, weren't the head coach. The brothers Kubiak are all legends in the relatively small pond that is Michigan football. Bob and Ken, the elders, played at Olivet College and distinguished themselves on the semipro circuit while Tim played collegiately at Toledo, in the Mid-American Conference.

I ask Ken if the allocation of the starting role will cause friction in the family.

"The rest of the family was a little pissed because they know my work ethic . . ." he stops short of saying something he might regret about his brother. I am struck by his sheer competitiveness. About how this can mean so much to a thirty-nine-year-old with other things going on. About this, however, I am a little jealous. I went from it meaning way too much (college, high school) to it meaning a little too little now. It is another assignment and I'm looking at it as a writer would.

"It's interesting, it's fun, and it's something that a lot of people would never get a chance to do," says Bob Kubiak, when I ask him about coaching his brothers at media day, the night before our game. Aside from a newspaper reporter or two, I think I am the only "media" present. This doesn't bode well. Bob is tall, with a balding head of gray hair, cut short, and a goatee. Unlike most coaches, he has a friendly face.

"There are a lot of good things, and there are lifetime memories that come with it. But there's stress. There's stress involved. But we come from a football family with five brothers who all played football. If you're a coach you've gotta be able to make a decision and stand by it. Both of my brothers know it's a hard decision and it can be uneasy. Sometimes you don't agree with all of the decisions but you work hard and make the best of it.

"The number-one thing both of them have is competitiveness. They both want to play, they both want to start, and they both want to be the best at what they do. They both have strong arms. Basically the decision I made is that Tim is a little bit younger and he has the more recent experience. But if you look at both of them at practice it's hard to see a difference between either of them."

I ask Kubiak who else has stood out to him, in practice.

"Brian Dolph obviously brings some maturity and experience to his game along with being talented. Most of our guys are a little seasoned. Eric Gardner looks like a great player on both sides of the ball. Don Lonsway, a little receiver I played with in semipro, runs good routes and is a disciplined guy. You don't have to be a burner in this league and he's just hung around. I'm happy with the way the linemen are responding to Allsbury, the way they do the conditioning and accept criticism.

"But the roster that you see in week one will not be the roster that you see at the end of the year. It's going to be an evaluation process. We need a growth pattern here to see how this team develops through the course of the year."

Chuck Selinger walks in as I am wrapping up my interview with Kubiak.

"But we've gotta have a kicker . . . gotta find one," Kubiak says within earshot of Selinger, who doesn't lack for self-confidence. We all take a minute to look around at the arena.

"This is cool," says Kubiak. "It's good to be in the building."

"Which way is the locker room?" Selinger asks.

"It's that way," says Kubiak. "I was just in there . . . I didn't even believe they had one but it's got showers and everything."

The Astroturf arrives in rolls and is forklifted off a truck and onto the concrete floor of Kellogg Arena as I mill around with some of the players after the media day walk-through workout.

We're all too polite to say what we're thinking, as we bend down and grab pieces of turf, examining the threadbare surface and meager quarter-inch of decayed padding separating us from a date with concrete. The turf is not unlike the stuff that old people used to buy in hardware stores and put on their front porch to keep from slipping. What we're thinking, of course, is that this turf sucks.

"It's not as bad as the stuff we played on in Jackson," Gillette says, trying admirably to put a positive spin on the carpet. Tom Martinez, our team doctor, is less optimistic.

"Somebody's breaking a bone tomorrow," he says, adding, "I just hope it's not one of our guys."

Martinez is a young chiropractor, recently relocated in Battle Creek via Kansas City. He often brings his fiancée, a beautiful younger woman, to practice with him. Martinez, I learn, used to be a professional bull rider.

"I stopped the day after my son was born," he says. "I took him home from the hospital and then drove 110 miles so that I could go to a show. That was common for me back then. Anyway, as I was standing around waiting to ride I ended up pulling the 'money bull', which was the bull that everybody wants to get. When you spend some time around the circuit you begin to recognize which bulls you want to ride and which ones you don't. But as I was standing with some of the other riders, listening to the national anthem, one of the guys turns to me and says, 'Martinez you're white as a sheet'. So I got on the back of the bull and got tossed around a little bit and fell off. That was my last day as a professional bull rider."

Before we are interrupted, Martinez goes on to tell me about his bout with liver cancer, his divorce, and how he ended up here, in Michigan. I realize how much I have come to appreciate his conversational ability. I seek Martinez out for a chat before almost every practice, in an unspoken tradition that, I imagine, might be making this experience bearable for both of us. I ask him how he got involved with us in the first place.

"Well, I went from being a big, stupid jock, to being a doctor," he says, proud but not arrogant. "And the first thing I did as a physician was pronounce my stepfather dead, from a suicide."

"I met Mike Powell at a Chamber of Commerce luncheon when I was just trying to get established in town," he recalls. "I told him about my background in sports and to get in touch if he needed anything. That was the last I heard of him until he came into my office a few months later, when Azriel Woodson hurt his shoulder. Powell said, 'Why don't you come to practice tonight and we'll talk details?' I guess the rest is history. I agreed to come to games and practices, and treat the players for no cost throughout the season, in exchange for a full-page ad in the program, two banners, and PA announcements at all of the games."

Around us, Crunch reserve fullback Jacob Hoxie is leading his construction crew in the assemblage of the boards that we'll be crashing into in about forty-eight hours. Hoxie has been putting in eighteen-hour days on the project, he explains, and he is surrounded by lag bolts, plywood and two-by-fours on all sides, his Crunch T-shirt soaked with sweat. Hoxie is an emotional guy on the field—a yeller and screamer type who happens to also be married to the assistant general manager and director of the Illegal Motion dance team, Amanda Hoxie. Minor league football is a family affair.

Hoxie loves football, but a neck injury derailed his walk-on attempt at Michigan State, and he has since been playing sporadically for a semipro outfit called the Albion Chargers. Hoxie is a good, gritty semipro player but his body type, like mine, seems a little out of place in this game. There is no place for a fullback/linebacker who isn't the prototypical bowling-ball 260-pound type.

In three weeks, despite his efforts in hammering our field into existence, he will be gone.

I wheel the Echo past the chain restaurants along Twenty-eighth Street, and behind the inevitable Barnes and Noble Booksellers (where I am drawn in for a quick prepractice cappuccino) and finally pull into the Grand Rapids Rampage practice facility, which doubles as an indoor soccer place. I follow the *thud* of pads and the *chirp* of whistles, past photographs of floppy-haired West Michigan soccer players with names like Vandermuelen, and into the football section of the facility.

Already, the differences are obvious. The Rampage, a member of the Arena Football League (or the big leagues of indoor football) since 1998, have matching practice uniforms and the use of two full-sized field-turf fields on which to practice. They also have six coaches on the payroll, and for all of them it is a full-time gig. Andrew Lopusnak, the Rampage director of media relations, meets me here. As do all good PR men, Lopusnak has the right mix of "been there, done that" cynicism, coupled with a requisite awe of the athletes.

"Mike Vanderjagt kicked on this field!" he says, excitedly, while giving me a detailed history of the FieldTurf on which we stand (which came to the club via a defunct team called the Minnesota Fighting Pike, for whom Vanderjagt had a cup of coffee).

"The league minimum in the AFL is 26,500 dollars," he explains. "But all of the contracts are incentive-laden, meaning that the more games you play, the more touchdowns you score, the more dollars you can make. Tony Graziani (a sought-after quarterback for another club) just signed for 165,000 dollars per year, base."

I look at the players running through drills on the field. They look, physically at least, exactly like us, save for the fact that the uniforms are newer and nicer. In fact, I think I see one of our defensive backs, here on a two-day tryout. I will have to further investigate this later.

We make the mistake of stepping onto an auxiliary field, where the Rampage linemen and linebackers are working on pass-protection drills. I catch the eye of a fullback named Chris Ryan.

"No reporters on the field!" he shouts in my direction. I laugh uncomfortably and look at Lopusnak who also laughs uncomfortably. Coming in here was his idea in the first place and he makes no move for the door.

"Would the reporter in the rumply-ass jeans please leave the field!" shouts Ryan, again. Ryan has noticed, rightly, that my jeans could use a good pressing. I notice that he is at least a hundred pounds overweight for his height, and it's not muscle (the 224-page *Rampage Media Guide* reveals that he is a svelte 320 pounds and enjoys riding his motorcycle in his spare time). I think Ryan, himself, is rumpled. I ask Lopusnak about him.

"He was one of [owner] Jon Bon Jovi's favorite players when he was with the [Philadelphia] Soul," he says. "We paid big dollars for him."

"Is he worth it?" I ask. Lopusnak says something about leading the league in touchdowns a couple of years ago or something. And something else about how he worked his way up from little-known Clark College in Atlanta. A real inspirational story.

Ryan is still giving me the business as he walks off the field. I decide to be bold and extend my hand to him for a handshake.

"Ted Kluck, ESPN.com," I tell him.

"I know who you are," he replies, lying. Nobody knows who I am.

"Imagine having to coach him," says his position coach, having overheard our conversation.

The practice, which was remarkably laid-back for that of a losing team, is already over. It is 10 A.M. I ask Lopusnak what the players do for the rest of the day. He has to think about the question for a moment.

"They're pretty much on their own," he says, after some deliberation. "Some of the guys watch film, some of them lift weights."

It has been a number of years since I've been in a bowling alley. My ten-year high school reunion a couple of summers ago took place in a bowling alley bar but we never actually bowled. Our first "Meet the Team" event is scheduled for a Saturday afternoon, at a facility (Knottke's Fun Time Lanes . . . or Family Fun Center . . . or something) in Battle Creek. The dance team will be there, along with food and, we are told, actual fans.

Well, one out of three isn't bad. Entry into The Fun Zone reveals all of the comforting similarities of a bowling alley—nonexistent cavelike lighting and a prevalent odor of decades worth of cigarette smoke. If the government actually decides to make smoking illegal, I think smokers should just flee to bowling alleys, rather than caves, for amnesty.

After adjusting my eyes, I look around to find my teammates gathered around a high table with a couple of Crunch helmets on top. We each file by and sign the helmets, providing my first autograph dilemma, which I will explain later. There are no fans here yet, but I'm not worried because it's still a couple of minutes before start time. They'll show up.

There has been a bit of a bowling renaissance amongst pro athletes in recent years, led by Jerome Bettis and Terrel Owens, so much so that ESPN even ran a bowling series for a while in which athletes bowled against each other for cash. And as such we take to the lanes for bowling and banter. Sometimes I fear that we are just parodies or facsimiles of the professional athletes to whom we have access, thanks to twenty-four-hour-a-day feeds from ESPN, NFL Network, and others. We see them so often, hear their sound bites, hear them miked-up on NFL films, that I fear that we no longer have the ability to have our own personalities, rather, we are just combinations of the athletes we admire.

Coach Allsbury is sitting with a group of players and eyes me suspiciously as I approach. A former walk-on at WMU from Bronson, Michigan, Allsbury was on the 2002 Lombardi Award watch list in addition to being named to the 2000 and 2001 All-MAC First Team. I swallow hard and decide to break the tension.

"Hey Allsbury," I tell him. "I'm thinking of making your character a homosexual in the book." There it is, some good, derisive, culturally insensitive banter. Out of character for me, but whatever.

This produces a huge smile on his face and a laugh from the rest of the players. Mission accomplished. I slap him five and move on toward the bowling.

My teammates are surprisingly good bowlers. Not surprisingly, most of them are ultra-competitive and care very little for the fans (who still haven't shown up) or the atmosphere; they want to win. Selinger has his kid with him today, but organizes a foursome including me, Crunch PR guy Nate Adams, his son Clayton, and WR/LB L. J. Parker from Indiana University, who is probably our best athlete.

Parker passes the eyeball test. He has the look of an athlete, from the thickly muscled, slumping shoulders to the semiswagger of tight hamstrings and big quadriceps. He also has a perpetual look of boredom on his dark face, also a staple of the super athletic. It's a look that suggests that he has seen and done things (on and off the field) with his body that mere mortals such as myself could only imagine. And I believe the look. I like Parker. It's funny, now, in my second football life, I would rather be liked than feared or respected. In college, I was an ultra-intense, shaven-headed Allsbury-type warrior who stalked around with a perpetual scowl and didn't care if anyone liked me as long as I was the most intimidating guy on the field or in the weight room. Now it's the opposite, I would like to be liked by these guys.

Selinger is locked in an intense battle with the PR guy for bowling supremacy. They're both competitive type-A guys with good bowling form. The PR guy has his own ball, his own shoes, and even one of the fancy-looking hand/wrist braces for bowling. He cools his hands over the air vent after every throw (roll?) just like on TV. When I compliment him on his game (he beat both of us handily), he unstraps his wrist brace and explains that he "was sandbagging for us."

At one hour into the event there are still no fans present. I sneak a glance at owner Mike Powell, still standing with the helmets, looking like someone ran over his dog. I think he is finding the business of minor league ownership to be somehow less glamorous than he expected. His mood is lifted somewhat by the appearance of the Illegal Motion Crunch dance team, who have appeared with their official 2006 team calendars. Knowing what we all know about young girls, police blotters, and athletes, I find the name "Illegal Motion" to be a flirtation with disaster, like the guy who said that nothing could sink the *Titanic*. But that's just me.

The calendars are creating quite a buzz among the players because they are by far the most professional-looking piece of glossy correspondence produced by the team thus far. The photographer succeeded in turning a bunch of cute Midwestern girls into starlets for the shoot, which is really what this whole thing is all about, in a way. There are tabs on the bottoms of the calendars which, if broken, means that you have to pay the twelve-dollar fee to purchase. They are, apparently, selling like hot cakes up and down the bowling alley as bowlers more accustomed to seeing fifty-year-old chain-smoking women are suddenly brightened by the presence of nubile twenty-somethings.

Toward the end of the event, the first of the fans appears. They occupy the lane next to me and are the parents of one of the dancers, Kiersha Danke. Her mother has her hair dyed black and orange, Crunch colors, and is thrilled to talk football with someone. After bantering with the mother for a while, I ask the attractive young girl sitting next to her in hipster glasses how the dance team stuff is coming together.

"Oh, she's not the dancer," corrects her mother, immediately. The girl in the glasses and I sit there awkwardly, not knowing exactly what to say next.

It's All Happening

Chapter Six

Game 1: Battle Creek versus Port Huron

What does it feel like when a dream dies? Not so much the dream of winning, or even playing well, but the dream of being a part of a team based on your ability to perform rather than the fact that you happen to write for the biggest sports Web site in the world. Let's get some uncomfortable facts out of the way up front. We lost Friday night to a good Port Huron Pirates team in the Great Lakes Indoor Football League opener, and on a personal level I sucked (two long snaps, both of them bad, after snapping well in practice and warm-ups).

That game night happened at all is, in fact, a small miracle brought about by the efforts of Hoxie's construction company and the Crunch front office. Powell (who has probably aged decades in the last three weeks) had to scramble to buy turf at the last minute (after another source, an indoor team in Wisconsin, pulled out three days before opening night) and was up until 3:30 A.M. the night before the game, sawing and hammering dasher boards into existence with Hoxie. These are the realities of the minor league owner, who has to be either eternally optimistic or completely insane.

"If you wake up tomorrow wearing your Crunch jersey, you have a problem," said starting linebacker Carmell Dennis who, after thirty-six years is finally a professional athlete. His comments got laughs but quite honestly getting jerseys on the night before the game is still as exciting now as it was as a kid. The jerseys, although all of them are huge (I think Powell got a volume discount on size

XXL), are slick black silk and mesh creations with white numerals and orange wedges on the shoulders. Very sharp. The players react in different ways. Quarterback Ken Kubiak and I check our looks in the mirror because Kubiak is wearing a uniform for the first time in several years, and it is clearly a meaningful moment for him. I later laid mine out on the floor at home to look at it while listening to music, trying to conjure some old vibes. Ches and Darrell Johnson, on the other hand, spatted their shoes with orange tape and coordinated the color of their bandannas to the accent colors of our jerseys. Wide receivers are shameless in their vanity (but I only wish I could look so cool).

I end up trading helmets in the moment before the game with Lonsway, who prefers the face mask on my helmet to his. Rather than unscrew face masks at this point we just swap lids because we both wear the same size. The helmets are brand-new Adams Pro-Elites. It is by far the most comfortable helmet I have ever worn, and the only time in my career I have ever gotten a brand-new lid. I look it over. It is lighter than the Riddells I have worn in the past, and, for the moment, is blemish-free. I can see my reflection in the shiny black shell and run my fingers over the raised Crunch logo. Much of the equipment that was promised to us—shoulder pads, gloves, warm-up suits—has yet to arrive, but I am happy to have my helmet in hand.

But there are other details to worry about as game time approaches, such as Ashe who is perhaps the most intense human being I've ever met, and his comment about cutting my balls off if I flubbed a snap in the game. I *think* he was kidding.

"Let's get a prayer," shouts Coach Allsbury, as we mill around the locker room in the minutes before game time. As per my usual routine, I was about four hours early getting to the arena. I was dressed before everyone else, and whiled away the hours going to the bathroom and generally exhausting myself with nerves.

The prayer, even though to these guys it's just another pregame ritual like spatting shoes, is still a comfort. I feel, for the first time, as if I can't get through this on my own power, and for the first time that I am letting my Lord be a part of this—a bigger part than just a pregame good-luck charm. We get down on the hard concrete and hold hands.

"Short and sweet!" shouts coach Ashe. "I don't want any sermons . . . I don't even know who you heathens pray to anyway."

We run out of the tunnel and through smoke and strobe lights, the music pounding through our helmeted heads, just as we had seen on television and I'm sure, a million times in our own minds. I am truly buzzed and understand why this is such a hard drug for men to kick. You don't get this in the cubicle, or on the assembly line. There is real electricity in the room, which at age thirty is a hard thing to generate. Lined up for the national anthem, helmets under our right arms, I look down the line and realize how long most of my teammates have waited for this. Many have played several years of semipro; some had small stints in big leagues and are working their way back up.

The game starts well, with Crunch WR Eric Gardner (who bears a striking resemblance to Apollo Creed) collecting the opening kick-off and ripping upfield for a 50-yard kickoff return for a touchdown, after which I skip my first snap back to Donnie Lonsway who gets it down for a good PAT. Bending over the ball, I feel a rush of nerves and excitement like I've never felt before. The ball feels slick from the sweat on my hands against its cheap composite material.

After, there is a series of miscues that lead to Port Huron touchdowns. Our offense is marked by Tim Kubiak being flushed out of the pocket and forced to run for his life, resulting in sacks, fumbles, and interceptions. The Pirates second score comes via a Terrell Thomas 20-yard fumble return for a touchdown, followed quickly by an Ernie Smith 46-yard interception return for a TD. On our next series, they add an Eddie Bynes safety, for good measure, to go up 24–7 in the first quarter. We are, in the realest sense, getting our dick strings knocked loose.

Our ineptitude also gives Franzer, who I don't think we laid a hand on all night, plentiful opportunities to start drives in good field position, resulting in touchdown passes to former UM standout Chris Matsos and professional indoor veteran Rayshawn Askew.

On my second snap (an extra point following a Kubiak TD strike to Eric Gardner) I almost get my friend Selinger killed, for which I will feel horrible the rest of the night. The snap was a dribbler, which bounced directly into the feeble Selinger's arms before he was summarily crushed by a group of Pirates defenders. I feel like hiding, so I take a place at the end of the bench with some of the injured players who still exist, but who exist at a much less noticeable level tonight. My wife gives an encouraging wave but all I can do is shake my head and turn around.

To long snap in a professional game is to experience tunnel vision. My whole life becomes a game of down and distance. As the offense sputters, I look at our position on the field to see if a field goal would be realistic, and begin to jockey for position by the door that opens through the padded dasher boards and onto the field. Once on the field I grip a composite football (cheaper than leather) that has become greased-pig slick with sweat. I grip the ball, suddenly nervous about doing what I have done to near-perfection in practice. Bryan Pittman, an NFL snapper for the Houston Texans who I talk to periodically, says he doesn't get nervous. I envy him. I peer back between my legs to the holder who raises his hand and gives a set call, and within seconds the chaos begins. Ideally, the snap is good and you hear the thud of the kicker's boot against the ball, and look up to see it sailing through the uprights.

L. J. Parker, the converted WR from Indiana, makes a ton of plays from his "Mac" LB position and ends up being one of our few bright spots. He sprains a knee but battles on for the rest of the night. Our defensive backfield sustains injuries to some of its stars—Johnson, who plucked an interception out of the sky early in the game, would later be hobbled by a sprained ankle. And it would be

Ches running around catching passes and hammering opponents until the final gun, keeping the group together.

The second half offered more of the same—Franzer killing us on scrambles (he scores on runs of 2 and 26 yards, also tossing a TD pass to Darryl Frager) which never allows us to even get close. As the minutes tick by, we get a feel for Port Huron's personality as a team. They have spent big dollars to bring in studs from all across the nation (Franzer and Askew were league champions in a rival league last season, LB John Cousins played at USC) and are universally thought to have the most loaded roster in the league. This fact hasn't escaped their attention either, as they take every opportunity to wag a finger or lob a nugget of trash talk our way.

The game was captured by a moment near the end when Port Huron's highly touted running back Rayshawn Askew caught a long touchdown pass and proceeded to dance in our end zone and leap up on our boards to posture. I had an unhealthy and almost uncontrollable desire to knock him (this person I'd never met) off the boards and drive him, headfirst, into the concrete floor. Losing will do this to you.

After the game, there is the surreal experience of signing autographs for children, who for the most part have no idea that I am a marginal (at best) athlete. I strongly considered fleeing this scene completely; feeling like it would be too much work to explain things. But I just try to smile and sign T-shirts, footballs, programs, and water bottles for them, because children mercifully don't see bad performances in the box score; they just see a friendly face in a uniform.

I'm chatting on the field with Chris Gillette about how you really can't go back. Gillette is the 290-pound confectioner who owns and operates his own chocolate shop in Battle Creek when he isn't trying to punish opposing quarterbacks. In our memories the stands were always full, we always played great, looked great in our uniforms, and the team always won. That's the forgiving thing about memories and years that pass. To trifle with those things, in the interest of curiosity or just plain ego, is like exhuming dead bodies: a bad idea. But I look around—at Gillette who tore his rotator cuff (a painful shoulder injury) making a tackle tonight, L. J. Parker, Brian Dolph, Donnie Lonsway, Harry Pettaway, and the other guys—and realize what a privilege it was to battle with them and watch them play through pain in pursuit of their dreams. Many of them have to get up tomorrow, early, and go to their day jobs. I will think about the bad snaps for an hour on the way home, and for another couple of sleepless hours tonight. They will probably ruin the potentially good interactions I could have had with my family, who care very little about this and from whom I receive unconditional love. I will go back to practice on Monday, go through the agony of seeing the films, and then try to win my job back because that's what a professional would do.

Because for the first time in thirty years, after watching professional teams run out of tunnels, warm up under bright lights, and finally sign autographs afterward; I am one of them. Some of the guys, stung by the loss, shower and leave quickly, but most of us hang around in our uniforms until the last of the fans have left the field, cognizant of the fact that this won't last forever.

Game 2: Battle Creek Crunch versus Marion Mayhem

One of the things I'm enjoying most about these games is the weekly conversation I have with Doc Martinez on the bench. Typically, our conversations center around Doc and his relationships, because he is a single, thirty-seven-year-old wildly charismatic (that's for you, Doc) doctor in a new city. Things are bound to happen.

"I'm about to give up on women," he tells me, shaking his head. This ought to be interesting. Truth be told, talking with Doc on the sidelines really helps move the time along when I'm not playing, and it helps get my mind off how nervous I am when I do actually play.

"For whatever reason I've always dated younger women," he says. "I have pretty high standards, I like a beautiful girl." After a pause, he adds, "but I know it's an ego thing. It's all ego."

"Young girls are exciting," I tell him, trying to effect my best pop psychologist persona. "There's something hopeful about them. They're not jaded yet. They haven't figured everything out. But the thing about young girls, postcollege-aged girls in their early twenties, is that they're usually relentlessly selfish. Think about it, when was the last time one of these girls actually asked you about your life?"

Doc nods knowingly, as if I've hit upon a profound truth.

"I need that Teddy," he says. "I need them to stroke my ego a little bit."

"We all need that Doc," I reply, glancing up at my wife, who is here for no other reason than to stroke my ego. God knows she wouldn't be here of her own volition.

And it's an ego that needs stroking tonight.

Let's start from the beginning. My preseason workout partner and Crunch kicker Chuck Selinger calls an impromptu onside kick, which caroms out of bounds after dribbling along for 10 yards, and the Mayhem take possession on our 10-yard line. Bob Kubiak goes berserk—it's as berserk as I've seen Bob Kubiak go this year. He gets in Selinger's face as he comes off the field, screaming that he's the coach and he's the one who calls onside kicks. Selinger, ever the stoic, acts like this doesn't bother him but for the first time I realize that he might not be around next week.

Coach Ashe, who admirably is dealing with his own anger issues in a sort of self-administered Barnes & Noble–style Zen regimen, walks by and mumbles, "F'ing kicker."

Not a great start.

Nonetheless, we battle back with a long scoring strike from Tim Kubiak to Eric Gardner, who is quickly establishing himself as a star, and attempt to make a bit of history with the GLIFL's first ever drop-kick. I bend over the football for the PAT, breathing heavily and trying not to focus on the 600 pounds of Marion Mayhem lined up in each "A" gap to my right and left. The ball is a little slick because I have decided to snap without gloves today. My snap to Selinger is perfect; however, he shanks the kick badly, sending it wide right by about 15 feet.

There is more drama developing in the stands; one of our players has made the bold move of inviting his "baby-mama" (baby mama: the mother of one's children, not necessarily one's wife or even one's girlfriend) and his other girlfriend, who is seated just two rows in front of the baby-mama and the children. This will be an interesting situation to keep an eye on throughout the evening. Surprisingly, neither woman is glamorous, and they are both, in many ways, your typical young, Midwestern women. The baby-mama is in a T-shirt printed with her man's number, while the girlfriend's attire is more understated.

As games go, it was a good one. The final score was 37–34, Marion, and we were led by Tim Kubiak's four TD tosses to Eric Gardner.

At halftime we were up 20–7, and could taste our first win of the season. "These guys are soft," was the refrain that echoed around the locker room. Keep it up for thirty more minutes and we notch our first professional win.

Marion would rally in the second half, however, largely as a result of my bad snap. After an early third-quarter touchdown, I bend over the football as I have thousands of times in my life, to send a crisp, 7-yard snap back to the holder. The two huge Marion linemen are lined up across from me, shading either shoulder, and I grip the slick football and look back between my legs at Ken Kubiak and Chuck Selinger. I see Kubiak between my legs because my usual holder, Don Lonsway, was released this week, which I found out just hours before game time when he didn't show up. Kubiak gives the "set" call, and I wait a couple of seconds before "short arming" a bad snap in his direction, which caroms off the carpet and is deftly placed down by Kubiak. The good part, for me, is that the snap was fast and relatively accurate. The kick is blocked, however, and returned for a Marion TD by Kodi Lindsay. On the runback I am clipped in the back by one of their gigantic linemen, and sprawl face-first onto the turf, sustaining a nice, bloody burn on my right arm. I jog to the sidelines with my head down, so as not to make eye contact with the coaches.

Jeremy Werner scores on a 7-yard run with 4:42 left in the third quarter and Marcus Allen hauls in a 16-yard TD pass from Corlew and returns a fumble 32 yards for a score to complete the Marion comeback. We are coming apart.

After another touchdown, I grab my helmet and begin jogging out onto the field to join the extra-point team. I am stopped by a large, meaty hand on the front of my shoulder pads.

"Not him!" I hear Kubiak scream, about me. "He's too damn small!" I pull off my helmet and walk back to the sidelines, where I will sulk for the rest of the game. I will walk immediately to the locker room after shaking hands with the Mayhem, who are a pretty decent bunch of guys. I will not return to sign autographs, and will take the service entrance out to my car because I don't want to see anyone. I hate this feeling.

"That hurts," says Chris Gillette, the big tackle who is out with an injury. "He [Kubiak] didn't have to do it like that."

My cell phone rings this morning and it's Chuck Selinger, informing me that he has been released, after another kicker was brought in for a tryout in our last practice.

These tryout situations are always awkward. There's a new guy milling around, not talking to anybody, just trying to stretch or warm up on his own. The new guy is Brad Selent, a slight-looking character with wire-rimmed glasses and a receding hairline. Kickers. Nonetheless, Selent has credentials. He was All-MAC at Western Michigan, and last kicked for the Detroit Fury in the AFL.

They've brought in a long snapper, too, I learn, no doubt as a part of Allsbury's crusade to replace the writer. He thinks I suck and, in his defense, I haven't done much to prove him wrong lately. The new long snapper, Tyler Paesens, weighs about 320 pounds and is just lasering the ball back to the holder. He is sensational. I can see my job being taken away as I flip him ball after ball.

Finally I got an opportunity to snap and did some of my best snapping of the year, firing ball after ball accurately back to the holder in a cool drizzle. Trying not to look nervous, and trying to look professional as I approached the football each time.

I try to accentuate the positives, realizing that not snapping will, I hope, allow me some mental rest, a reprieve from the pressure, and a chance to focus on my writing. I glance back at Allsbury and he is enraptured with the new snapper, smiling like I imagine he would if someone came up and asked to feel his biceps.

After practice, the last thing I feel like doing is interviewing Bob Kubiak, but because I don't want to drive home feeling like I've accomplished nothing, I pull out the tape recorder. The stress of two losses has dampened his enthusiasm considerably.

"It's actually been more stressful than I thought . . . I took it on thinking, 'Hey, this is gonna be a good time, and my other college stuff is gonna be mellowed out in the off-season.' But personnel is a big issue . . . that got a little nitpicky. Trying to find and install an offense was tricky. I looked at a lot of tape of NFL teams, and I went up to Grand Rapids and sat with Sparky McEwen's staff and looked at film."

I ask Kubiak how the staff is working out.

"I know Scott Ashe's passion for this game. I don't think you can get more passionate about any avenue of football. He's got a toughness about him. Anthony Allsbury was lucky. I sold him his house and I knew his past. He's another guy that I would hire in a heartbeat on my college staff. You coach hard, you get into people but you want to have a good time. This isn't everybody's livelihood."

Thank God, or I would have just lost my job.

Ridin' Dirty

Chapter Seven

Just because you are a character, doesn't mean
you have character.

—The Wolf, *Pulp Fiction*

We have our own Wolf now, an assistant coach, Dave Wolf, who has been hanging around the last couple of weeks and goes by the moniker. He has set up shop in the back of the bus, which has become a cross between Bourbon Street and the Las Vegas strip. Only the strong dare to venture back there. I have settled someplace in the middle— not as cool as the back, but also not as lame as the front of the bus, where the ownership and Battle Creek Crunch team staffers sit by default.

I can almost gauge down to the minute how long it takes our serious drinkers to get drunk, and how long it will be before the insults begin. They, the insults, are always the same—always something about how (insert name) "sucks cock" or his "mom sucks cock." These phrases are always yelled at the top of one's lungs, and then laughed at like it's the first time anybody has ever heard it. This is life on a bus, with a professional football team. Glamorous. It makes me think that if this is what it means to be an elite, or nearly elite, athlete, that I hope my son just stops playing after high school.

Just a few minutes into the ten-hour trip to Rochester there are already problems. We signed a talented defensive back that the team immediately named "White Ches" in honor of his small stature and striking (but Caucasian) resemblance to WR/DB Chesaurae Rhodes.

Unfortunately White Ches isn't with us. There has been a mix-up in communication and we will have to pick him up at a gas station somewhere off Interstate 94 near Ann Arbor, making an already miserably long trip longer. To add to the drama, dedicated practice player Jacob Hoxie has been told that he will be able to dress if White Ches doesn't materialize. Hoxie practically begins putting on his gear when he hears the news, but deflates visibly when White Ches ambles onto the bus. Player turnover is a hard reality of life in the low minors.

After stopping for dinner at an all-you-can-eat buffet outside of Cleveland, defensive end Harry Pettaway, one of our older players, puts *Crash* in the DVD player attempting to interject a little bit of culture into the proceedings. Gradually, the shouts and insults hurled from one end of the bus to the other stop as a busload of boozy players, both black and white, process what they are seeing. I look around the bus and realize that most of the guys from our week one roster are gone, with only the brothers Kubiak, L. J. Parker, Kyle Lacksheide, Black Ches, Eric Gardner, and Pettaway remaining.

Several hours into the trip I wonder who we are. Are we really ourselves, or are we just an amalgamation of the millions of hours of bad football movies (*Any Given Sunday*, *The Program*) we watch on road trips, and the NFL Films mini-features on which we were weaned? We talk not in real conversations, but in octaves-lower sound bites, saying what we think football players are supposed to say. On hour seven of the trip, somewhere in the rolling hills of eastern Pennsylvania, this disturbs me, probably more than it should.

I spend most of the trip talking quietly across the aisle with L. J. Parker, who has become the closest thing I have to a true friend on the club. He is telling me about his children—two little girls—who he cares for during the day, and about his problems with their mother. He is trying to do the responsible thing, he says, by working and trying to get a shot playing football. Parker was a highly recruited WR out of Ottawa Hills High School in Grand Rapids, and chose to play at Indiana under offensive guru Cam Cameron. When

Cameron was replaced by Gerry DiNardo, however, Parker was replaced as well.

"DiNardo didn't recruit me, so DiNardo didn't want me," he tells me, through the darkness. He then went to NAIA's St. Francis University in hopes of a transfer, and after completing their summer practices, was told he was ineligible. After a tryout with the Grand Rapids Rampage he finds himself here. At the end of the football world.

"I just need to get me three years on an NFL roster," he says. "Then I qualify for the pension."

Rolling through northern Ohio, on a bus with twenty-five other drunks, three years on an NFL roster seems as far away as the moon.

I think of Kristin often on the road—taking every excuse to pull out my obnoxious little cell phone (hidden in the pants pocket—not hanging off the belt like some ridiculous corporate superhero) and give her a call.

She saved me really. When I was gaunt and wasting and rudderless in college she nursed me back to health with love and a steady diet of Salinger, Dumas, Austin, Steinbeck, and the Bible. She taught me to read. I knew how to read words on the page before—I was in college for crying out loud—but my idea of "serious" reading was Rick Reilly's column on the back page of *Sports Illustrated*.

I first saw her in a reader's theater on the poems of Chicago poet Carl Sandburg. She was the shortest girl onstage, which combined with her cherubic (forgive the cliché) features made her stand out. I liked that she was not the prototypical tall, blonde, rich, Dutch, trust-fund princess that Taylor enrolled in droves.

I was there for a class—although I can't recall which—and had every intention of slinking out during the first intermission after I had successfully scored enough sketchy notes with which to complete a paper. This was customary of my after-hours school commitments. "It's my time," I reasoned. That logic still made sense.

But I stayed in my seat. The girls wore blood-red velvet gowns and spoke the mighty Sandburg's words with anger and passion—very un-Taylorlike qualities that I could relate to at the time.

".. . She liked blood-red poppies for a garden to walk in . . ."

"The red drips from my chin . . . I came from killing, I'll go to more . . ."

".. . like a child cries for its suck mother, I cry for war."

They spoke of things raw, aggressive, and masculine.

The Wolf and the rest of the guys have paired off and gone their separate ways for the evening, to sample the best of what Rochester nightlife has to offer. I am burned out on people and make my way outside the Doubletree Hotel where I run into team intern Sean Lalonde who is clearly burned out as well. Unfortunately, football teams tend to devour the weak, and much of their derision is directed at Sean. Yet, I increasingly feel like he is probably the glue that is holding the whole thing together. He asks my opinion of the experience thus far.

"I think I would be happy just coming back every year to practice and play in one game," I tell him, bemoaning the bus travel, time away from family and day-to-day physical pounding. "Just to go out, put the uniform on, and prove that I can still take the shots."

I have been trying to enjoy some of football's more sublime pleasures in the last weeks—putting on the helmet and jersey each day for practice, jogging out onto the field on a perfectly cold spring night, and the thrill of squaring off against players who have been in The Show.

"Well," he says, stamping out a cigarette, "you definitely took some shots."

Game 3: Battle Creek versus Rochester

After spending our six-dollar per diem on breakfast at Burger King (we decided Perkins was out of our price range) we spend the majority of game day just killing time. New kicker Brad Selent and I watch the World Trick Shot Billiards Championships on ESPN6 in the morning. If you're wondering "who in the world watches that crap" it's us—nervous athletes trying to kill time.

In the afternoon we make our way, as a group, to a local movie theater where the plan was to watch a Bruce Willis action flick—lots of killing and car chases to get us in the proper frame of mind. We end up seeing a film called *Madea's Family Reunion*, which is a strange mix of comedy (Tyler Perry cross-dressing as a foul-mouthed grandmother) and earnestness (a spousal abuse subplot complete with soaringly cheesy ending). It's the kind of movie that makes you want to reach for a box of tissues. It doesn't exactly make you want to go out and hit somebody in the face.

As a player I have had my own ups and downs, but mostly downs. I started at long snapper in our first two games (both losses) only to lose my job this week to a bigger (320 pounds to my 210), and better snapper (he snaps like he's not thinking about snapping). I found out, for sure, that I wouldn't start the night before the game at the hotel bar.

Not starting gives me an opportunity to appreciate Rochester's game day atmosphere. The well-lit arena is soon full, and music pounds through the sound system as we warm up.

Rock and roll is one of the most underratedly satisfying things about being an athlete. Let me explain: Ask any athlete and they will equate different songs with different stages of their careers. Songs are blared over the PA during warm-ups and in the locker room before the game. Rock and roll—full of testosterone-driven, aggressive adolescent fury—goes hand in hand with football.

Van Halen's "Runnin' with the Devil" will always take me back to Tipton High School—home of the Blue Devils—in 1993. It was a dusky, early fall Friday night. The school released a bunch of blue and silver balloons into the sky while we warmed up to this song. They had a gravestone with our school's name planted in their end zone, and a team full of stud athletes. It was the day I knew I arrived as a varsity football player. We lost but I hung tough. I'll always love that song.

"Symphony of Destruction" by Megadeth will always bring me into the inside of our locker room, in my junior year of high school. Whitey—Kevin Whitesell, who at age eighteen had a full chest of hair and looked older than my father—brought in his sound system, cranked the album, and generally stalked around looking sinister. He wore a black visor on his helmet which the coaches promptly removed after our first loss. Metal lockers painted red. Coaches and players pacing around, getting ready for battle or peeling off wet jerseys after a victory. There was always music after a win and stone silence after a loss. Commandment Number 1 in football: never have fun after a loss.

More recently, it was "Black Balloon" by the Goo Goo Dolls. It was the middle of the fourth quarter of my first game as a semipro ballplayer back in 1999. I was exhausted—I had played both ways as a linebacker and tight end. There was a time-out on the field and this song came on over the loudspeaker. I soaked it in because I knew that my wife was in the stands and I could still play. I felt every bruise and I loved life that afternoon.

Even now, when I go to stadiums to cover college and pro games I seldom envy the athletes. I don't envy the hours they spend poring over film and sitting in boring meetings. I don't envy the 6 A.M. workouts, or hours spent soaking away pain in the training room. I do, however, envy the warm-ups—the rock and roll, the testosterone pouring out of the stadium speakers whipping the fans into a frenzy. And you, in your shiny plastic helmet and clean jersey, ready to slay lions and entertain the masses. There are few days when I wouldn't trade it all for one more afternoon in the sun.

Not playing tonight also gives me a chance to experience a game day without the gut-wrenching nerves that usually accompany it. As we stand in the tunnel that leads to the field before the game, an older man pushes his way through the crowd of players with several Raiders front-office types. The old man gazes up at 6-foot-4, 275-pound Crunch DE Brian Wright and says, "If I were younger I'd kick the shit out of you." We all get a chuckle out of the old man and later learn that he is former boxing champion Carmen Basilio.

The game soon proves to be more of the same for us, however, as our kicking problems continue. New kicker Brad Selent has nearly every one of his kicks blocked—chalk it up to a low ceiling and porous blocking up front.

"Well, you can feel good about the fact that it wasn't your fault," says backup QB Kenny Kubiak on our way into the locker room at halftime.

As has been the case all season, our defense keeps us in the ball game. We have found a consistent pass rush in coach-turned-player Anthony Allsbury and WR-turned-LB-turned-DE L. J. Parker who has been our most reliable defensive performer. And despite a two-touchdown performance from WR Richard Gills and a five-catch, one-TD game from new signee Herb Haygood who played in the NFL with Denver, Kansas City, and Tampa Bay, the game slips away from us in the second half because Rochester's better-conditioned team simply outguns us. Our offense is having trouble making its calls and hearing the snap count as well because Rochester's ESL Center plays a bit like a night club—loud hip-hop music pounds through the arena before, during, and after plays. Raiders backup quarter-back Matt Cottengim, in his first professional start, went 16/25 for 212 yards and five touchdowns. Crunch QB Tim Kubiak threw four of his own touchdowns, but added four interceptions.

"We need to get more consistency out of Tim Kubiak," says brother Bob after the game. White Ches also has his problems, giving up two quick touchdowns and bobbling a kickoff in his own brief action. Sadly, I think it is the last we'll see of him.

As we stream off the field at the end of the game I am confronted by a large man who has a Tony Soprano look about him (however, the same could be said of many of the men in upstate New York, so take that with a grain of salt). The man is resplendent in a tailored suit and pumps my hand vigorously.

"Ted Kluck, thank you for the articles and thanks for what you're doing," he says. It finally clicks for me that he is Raiders owner Dave McCarthy, and I learn that he is something of a local legend, who is passionate about Rochester football.

"The best thing about this," he says, "is compiling a team with talent purely from the Rochester area. I mean it's one thing to offer guys housing and jobs and bring in a bunch of ringers from around the country like Port Huron, but it's another thing to win in Rochester with Rochester guys."

I ask him who he has been most impressed with, thus far.

"Our quarterback Omar Baker is obviously a great player; Dave Kallfelz, who was in an NFL camp with the Chiefs, should get a shot at the next level; and Noah Fehrenbach should definitely be in an NFL camp."

Cottengim seemed to throw TDs at will in the second half, often connecting with WR Fehrenbach who pulled off perhaps the coolest end-zone celebration I have ever seen—climbing the wall to perform a WWE–style elbow drop onto the football.

Lest we thought we wouldn't miss Doc Martinez, who didn't make the trip for personal reasons, our postgame locker room looks like a MASH unit, with Kevin Smith groaning in pain because of a knee injury and linebacker Azriel Woodson bandaging his own grotesquely disfigured toe. Woodson had the toenail ripped off early in the game. I find him sitting alone, next to a stack of pizza boxes, in an auxiliary locker room. He smiles and extends a hand. I ask Woodson, who I wouldn't have pegged as the reflective sort, if he has any regrets about getting involved this season.

"Gas money," he says without hesitation. Woodson is from Detroit, yet has been a regular at evening practices. "They promised me gas money and I haven't seen it yet." I learn that Woodson works near the Detroit Airport for Federal Express, and that his coworkers don't know that he moonlights as a professional football player. I also find that, in this setting, away from the rest of the players, he is kind and thoughtful. He adds, "We missed the Doc tonight. I hope this is the last time we travel without him."

Before getting on the bus I witness my first groupie sighting at this level, as L. J. Parker and Eric Gardner entertain a pair of young

Rochester ladies in the darkness near the bus. It all looks very inno-cent, the guys standing around waiting for the bus to leave, the girls giggling. But it looks, to me, like the experience makes them feel more like true professional athletes, as groupies, to this point, were a piece of the puzzle that had remained unplaced. Parker, with his dark good looks and huge smile, strikes me as the kind of guy who could pick up a girl anywhere.

Watching Parker makes think about the underlying sexuality inherent in every sports situation I have ever been involved in. Un-fortunately, I have become very much desensitized to the whole thing after being a part of it for so long. A virgin until marriage, I'd always just laughed uncomfortably and tried to blend in when the topic of "getting some" rolled around in the locker room—as it did on an almost daily basis. Teammates would approach each other, spin tales of conquest and then resume the business of preparing to hit one another on the field. Although the stories were interesting, in much the same way one may look at a Jerry Springer episode playing in a bus station waiting room, they all got a little humdrum after a while. But it led me to the conclusion that sex, violence, and narcissism all went together and were pretty much the main ingredients in the athletic soup that nourished me for so many seasons.

We see and use ourselves as objects, I thought, so why expect it to be any different with women. Athletes, used to being stripped bare and examined before the start of any season or as a part of the pro scouting process, are by college very much used to thinking of them-selves as machines or objects, and the whole thing had a very desen-sitizing effect, right down to the places we lived—the locker rooms, the dorms with other athletes—with sex being the prime topic of thought and conversation. As football players we're aggressive and proficient physically, which somehow translates into sexual irrespon-sibility in many cases. The fact that many sex crimes on college cam-puses are perpetrated by athletes is, along with academic failure and overall thuggery, a dirty little secret generally kept quiet by the NCAA.

Yet for people so well versed in supposedly attaining sexual gratification, most of the athletes I knew were horrible at relationships. Football bred a sort of narcissism fueled by egocentricity. Players are commodities that seek to be praised. All the objectification of them as interchangeable parts leads to a mentality that also devalues women. It is a self-fulfilling prophecy in which athletes feel that their only contribution to society is through athletics, and they continue to objectify themselves and others. This, of course, is good for business. And football, as is everything else, is all about the bottom line. Not the development of young men as so hopefully states the line in the admissions brochure.

As we kill the final minutes before the bus loads and leaves, after the girls have gone, Parker picks up a ball and begins running around on the artificial turf, seeming to never tire of playing the game. He flings the ball to no one—the rest of us are occupied with conversations and cell phone calls—and simply jogs over to retrieve it, the picture of happiness and contentment.

On the bus ride home there is not much to say after the 63–28 loss, the swagger and hope of the previous day's ride all but gone. Players use the time to ice their various injuries and some, including Parker who sits across the aisle from me, moan audibly at the acute pain of muscle cramps.

After the requisite gas station stop for beer (there was some controversy as to whether the Speedway sold cases of cold beer, causing a near mutiny) there are more football movies to be watched, and somebody throws in *Friday Night Lights*. In it, there is an awkward scene in which a reporter attempts to interview stone-silent DE Ivory Christian, who reacts to each question with a blank stare. I reach across the dark aisle and tap Parker on the shoulder.

"That's how I feel trying to interview you, Park," I tell him.

He is silent for a moment but through the darkness I think I see a smile.

"Our kicking game is killing us," Parker says, after a moment. "The offense kind of picked it up tonight . . ."

The offense is streaky, I tell him.

"It's not streaky; tonight is the first time they did anything," he says. "We gotta stay away from the officials too. Personal fouls are killing us. Everybody needs to worry about themselves. Do what they do."

We agree that the officials sucked, which, I guess, is to be expected from a new league.

"But I'm having fun doing what I do. I had fun with the fans and everything."

We ride on in silence for several minutes.

There is a scene I love at the end of *Friday Night Lights*, a scene that I think says everything about the nature of football. In it, the head coach is sitting alone at his desk, pulling the names of the departing seniors off a magnetized board, and throwing them in a box. Next year there will be somebody else in my uniform, somebody else wearing number 25. That somebody will be bigger, faster, stronger, and, most important, younger, than me. It's something that will eventually happen to everybody on this bus, sooner rather than later for most of us. Next week for some of us. It's something nobody wants to think about.

Herb Haygood played wide receiver at Michigan State University from 1998 to 2001, and then spent 2002–2003 with the Denver Broncos and 2004 with the Kansas City Chiefs. He has the second-most kick-return yards in MSU history and was part of a formidable WR duo that included Charles Rogers. He was a fifth-round draft choice in the 2002 NFL draft.

Today he is clad in a Battle Creek Crunch helmet (we signed him before the Rochester game) and an Albion Chargers (semipro) practice jersey, and is lined up across from me in a scrimmage period. Due to low attendance numbers and injuries, I am playing the "jack" linebacker position, which is really a hybrid OLB/Free Safety who often ends up covering WRs. I can see that Haygood is chewing gum through the bars of his face mask and his dark face, as always, is impassive. Herb Haygood never seems surprised, excited, or taken off guard by anything.

We are wearing shoulder pads and helmets today, which means that there will be some contact. I give Haygood a considerable cushion, a nod to his superior ability and speed, as well as my general lack of confidence in my ability to backpedal, "flip my hips," and run with the speedy receiver. He says nothing after each of our plays, except once to explain that he could "draw these guys [coaches] some plays that would score every time."

I asked Haygood why he signed with us. Why, after making six figures per season in The League, would he come out and sacrifice his body for two hundred bucks a game here?

"I was sitting in the stands at your first two games," he said. "I thought to myself, 'I can do that.'"

Just being on the same field and running with Haygood gives me confidence, and I try a jam technique—where the defensive back lines up tight and uses his arms and shoulders to tie up the receiver as he comes off the line of scrimmage. Shockingly, the technique works, and I manage to tie Haygood up near the line of scrimmage, taking him out of the play. He jogs back to the huddle and, as is customary, says nothing.

"You gonna try to jam me up again?" he asks, settling into his position for the next play. I say nothing, but feel a little quease of nerves coming on. At the snap, Haygood jukes me and throws on a quick "swim" move, before flying up the field to gather in the ball. All I hear is the *swoosh* of nylon on his jersey as he runs past, collecting the ball and running untouched across the goal line.

I'm stuck in Folsom Prison, and time keeps draggin' on.
—Johnny Cash, "Folsom Prison Blues"

I board the bus at 9:55 A.M., because we are scheduled to leave at 10:00, only to find a few players—Richard Gills, L. J. Parker, and Herb Haygood—in the back of the bus.

"Where is everybody?" I ask. Haygood shrugs his shoulders and pulls a blanket up around his shoulders. He has scored the prize spot on the chartered cruiser—a row of back-row seats that face a row of seats facing backwards—perfect for sleeping. I ask Herb, who looks and seems perpetually sleepy, his impressions of this experience, after having played in The Show.

"It's disorganized," he says, with no hesitation. "In the NFL we got a ninety-dollar-a-day per diem, and they also took care of dinner and a free movie at the hotel. Plus, in the league if the bus leaves at ten, it leaves at ten and if you're not on it you get fined. But I'm just doing this for fun," he says, "I don't really want to play anymore."

The players are concerned because, in addition to half the team, nobody has seen owner Mike Powell, who has been increasingly absent in recent weeks.

"If the owner don't come, we don't eat," says Gills, a new WR from Northwood University who had a brief stint in the AFL with the Grand Rapids Rampage.

"If he comes we still might not eat!" replies L. J. Parker. Parker was reprimanded by the team for calling repeatedly about the first game check, which arrived several weeks late.

"He never returned my calls," says Parker. "I don't know how many times I waited through *that Monday Night Football* ringtone. He's wasting minutes on that!"

"The owners are supposed to pay for housing, food, gas, and all that stuff," says Azriel Woodson, the moody linebacker who rarely speaks, but when he does is often scathing. Some of the other players have communicated that they think Woodson is cocky or arrogant—I think he's just quiet. "I'm only coming to one practice a week," declares the LB from Detroit. "It's 135 miles there and back. Have you seen the gas prices? Plus, I heard them cats in Port Huron got housing." Woodson is rolling now. "I heard that if a team can't continue financially, the league would help them out—paying salaries and all of that stuff."

The players nod somberly. I have with me a marketing book compiled by my agent, Mike O'Brien, for this year's NFL draft. O'Brien is less my agent (Who would want to represent such a hopeless athletic case as myself?) and more a friend. He has decided to build his agency on the Christian values of honesty and integrity—two descriptors not often used in conjunction with the sports representation business. I signed the official NFL "Standard Representation Agreement" at a cookout at O'Brien's house last summer, after I first shared my plan with him. I have since learned how tough it is to eke out a living swimming with sharks. O'Brien has been lied to by athletes' parents, been extorted for thousands of dollars in "certification fees" by the NFL Players Association, and basically been rebuffed at every turn by the high-profile twenty-one-year-olds that are the primest of the prime meat each year at the NFL draft.

The players are all eager to take a look at O'Brien's book because most of them have no representation. The book is glossy and slick, and was prepared for Zach Strief, a Northwestern lineman who ended up going elsewhere for representation. For the second-straight year, O'Brien was shut out of the NFL draft—honesty and integrity being tougher sells than he anticipated.

It is interesting to me to assess the reading material on the bus. Backup QB Kenny Kubiak always has an assortment of newspapers. There is always a stack of *FHM* and *Maxim* magazines floating around, although their origins are unknown. These are the types of soft-porn titles (called "lad mags" in the business) that carry pictures of women so fake-looking that they almost look like another species. Like they come from a different planet where the only inhabitants are beautiful, empty-eyed women, aged eighteen to twenty-five, who are perpetually washing cars and taking showers together.

"Hey Kluck!" shouts Carmell Dennis from the front of the bus, "this is the kind of magazine you need to be writing for!"

"It beats traveling with you knuckleheads," I shout back, good naturedly. This is good for me—Mello thinks I'm cool. As the saying goes, though, I don't think *Maxim*'s readers pick it up for the articles.

Having finished the novel *Sideways*, I am reading a book called *Exodus*, which describes the flight of Americans away from so-called "progressive" churches, back to Orthodox churches—the reason being that people want a religion that is demanding of them and requires them to be different, which is largely a Biblical premise. Azriel Woodson glances at the cover and nods his head in understanding. Some of the players call Wooodson "The Preacher" but I have yet to discuss religion with him, because, quite frankly, I find him a little intimidating. He sits with his back turned to the movies and shows little interest in drinking with the rest of the players. For most of the trip he has his ear glued to a cellular phone and mumbles things into it which are intelligible only to the party on the other line. After some fishing in a backpack he produces a title by T. D. Jakes, a Texas pastor who has built a megachurch and a publishing empire by largely catering to high-profile celebrity athletes such as Deion Sanders and Evander Holyfield. It's really only a handful of black players who would admit to even dabbling in religion, and most of these are fans of Jakes's motivational follow-your-dreams brand of gospel.

"Jakes is big," says Woodson, as I look through the book. "He's probably the third-biggest evangelist in history, behind Bobby Graham . . . I mean Billy Graham, and his kid." He says this as though he is discussing a lineup of Hall of Fame running backs.

Game 4: Battle Creek versus Marion

Marion, Ohio, is a small, blue-collar town in central Ohio, and as the bus winds its way through town, many of our black players are skeptical that it actually contains a pro football team.

"Black people don't live out here," says Gills. "I wouldn't play down here for all the money in the world."

The bus rolls past wide-open spaces, green fields, and the occasional farmhouse.

"Black people can't live out here," says Woodson. "It's too far from the gas station. We just put five bucks in and roll." As we approach downtown Marion, Woodson's interest is piqued by a gas station, offering prices of $2.74 per gallon. "Man, their gas is cheap here!" he says, excitedly, furthering his obsession with gas prices. I consider calling him Alan Greenspan, as a joke, but then think the better of it, figuring that nobody would get the reference.

These road trips foster an unintentional study of gas stations and their cuisine. Most of them are the same—cases of cold beer, a rough-looking but slightly flirtatious female clerk suddenly buoyed by the presence of twenty young, athletic men. Harry Pettaway, a fitness freak, always seeks out the PowerBar-type protein supplements. The rest of the linemen load up on pork rinds, Doritos, and pop. Ken Kubiak and I always get a bag of Combos—the snack industry's little miracle (cheese wrapped in a pretzel—wow). L. J. Parker always comes back to the bus with a bag full of candy (Skittles, Mike and Ikes, and the like), which he downs quickly, but never deviates from the 4 percent or so of body fat on his physique. I hate him for this.

I begin to get excited as we move toward the arena. At the last gas station I had a discussion with Coach Ashe, who explained that he is considering using me at nose tackle tonight, whether or not we are blowing the other team out. I am filled with excitement and fear, thinking that I might get my first taste of real, non-long-snapping action of the year. I played DE and DT in college, I explained to Ashe, when I was about thirty-five pounds heavier. Still, I think I can be effective shooting the gaps at nose, in the indoor game where the running game is not as much of a factor.

Veterans Memorial Coliseum in Marion is located on their fairgrounds, which are straight out of my county-fair memories. The bus wheels us past hog barns and a jalopy dirt-track complete with rickety bleachers. I suddenly feel a huge pang of nostalgia for my hometown in Indiana, where scenes like this are plentiful.

Adjacent to the arena is the Bank One beef pavilion, where there is some sort of a horse show happening. The players are largely quiet, the pregame nerves beginning to set in. It is nearly three and there was no lunch on the bus ride, which has some players skeptical.

"We gonna get baloney sandwiches without the baloney," says Gills.

We are finally led off of the bus and into the arena, where dust from the parking lot and the surrounding horse barns makes the air look hazy. The arena itself is impressive though, with the field surrounded on four sides by high walls and old, wooden arena seats. We get the impression that this barn is going to rock tonight. There are Marion Mayhem banners stretched over the exposed walls, and brand new Astroturf on the field. For the second week in a row we have turf-envy as we walk through plays on the cushiony (relatively) bright-green surface. Marion also looks to have sold an impressive number of sponsorships—every exposed surface seems to bear a corporate logo. This is how one makes money in minor league sports.

"At least their walls are all the same color," says Woodson. Eric Gardner, our enigmatic WR/RB/CB has found an outlet over one of the dasher board pads, so that he can charge up his omnipresent iPod. Eric Gardner marches to his own drummer, and that drummer, I think, plays continuously through his headphones.

"That E.G. is a little different cat," says Kenny Kubiak, who, like me, is watching the iPod charging experiment with interest. E.G. is expected to figure prominently tonight because Bob Kubiak, realizing that Gardner is his biggest talent, put in a new package of running plays to utilize his speed out of the backfield. Although the passing game has been abysmal, perhaps E.G.'s legs will carry us to glory.

The locker rooms themselves are tiny, and the team splits between rooms at either end of a long hallway. Strangely, most of the black players gravitate toward one room, while many of the white players go to the other. The rooms are a walk back in time—wooden dressing stalls, wooden folding chairs, drippy faucets, and old-school trough urinals. I imagine decades worth of rodeo cowboys and high school basketball teams dressing in here. Spitting their chewing tobacco in the sink and trying not to look scared, just like us.

"There were too many brothers in that other room!" Allsbury, who is of mixed race, announces as he bursts into our room. His comment gets a laugh from black and white players alike and breaks some tension over the cramped surroundings. There are the usual pregame dramas unfolding. Tyler Paesens, our big tackle, has left his shoulder pads at home and has parents speeding down I-75 to deliver his pads before kickoff. Chesaurae Rhodes is having trouble deciding whether to spat his shoes with orange or black tape. He is almost completely dressed in his uniform three and a half hours before kickoff. Allsbury shakes his head as Ches leaves.

"Dressed four hours before kickoff . . . I swear you would have trouble getting a 17 on the ACT with some of these guys combined," he says. "I'm always the last one to get dressed," Allsbury adds. "I like to be comfortable for as long as possible before the game."

I am beginning to get a read on Allsbury's pregame routine. First, he finds something trite to get pissed off about, in order to work himself into an adequate frenzy before game time. Today, it is the fact that he didn't get enough chicken cacciatore (delicious— great job Marion caterers) to eat at the pregame meal. He snapped at Bob Kubiak for going back for seconds. But Kubiak is a large man and could justify the seconds, as could Allsbury. He then sits in his locker stall for as long as possible, in his street clothes and just before it's too late, begins frantically ripping through his bag in search of his various uniform components. You may think that in the pros you just walk in to the dressing room and find your uniform hanging in the locker—but not so with us. We haul and pack all of our own gear, and there is no "backup supply" traveling with the club. Allsbury always forgets one or two items—a knee brace last week, and an Under Armour shirt this week, which causes him to unleash a stream of profanity. Just before game time he can be heard muttering an incoherent stream of cuss words that would make George Carlin blush. Just anger for anger's sake.

The rest of us are immersed in a riveting discussion on 1980s pro wrestling—reminiscing about our favorite characters and shows we saw as kids when wrestling was "pure." The players are loose and amiable today, which gives me the feeling that we actually have a shot at beating Marion tonight. They barely beat us the last time we played three weeks ago and we got the impression that they were a soft team due for a loss. Yet, they hung eighty-one points on the hapless NY/NJ Revolution last week.

"Tito Santana was my boy!" says Delano Harry, who has dressed for his first game tonight. "I like the acrobatic guys." Harry is a speedster, a college track star, from Wayne State University who had a two-day tryout with the AFL's Grand Rapids Rampage earlier in the year. Inexplicably, he has just been a practice player up to this point and tonight is his first real action in the Crunch uniform. He checks out his silky white number 13 jersey in the mirror.

Carmell Dennis, in the locker next to mine, performs a spot-on impression of "The Macho Man" Randy Savage. Dennis is buoyant, dressing again after being sent down for one game last week. He is a strong and versatile defender, able, at 260 pounds, to play linebacker or defensive end, as well as make contributions on special teams. But I know that Carmell is proud, and the call-ups and send-downs are wearing on him.

"Did you know that Savage and Lanny Poffo were brothers?" adds Harry Pettaway, who has been forced to dress in the shower area due to a lack of space. Pettaway is the "heaviest" traveler on the team— always bringing with him whatever extra equipment and exotic balms and training materials he can fit in his luggage.

"Poffo's the guy that used to read poetry and throw out the Frisbees," I add, my first contribution to the discussion. As a less significant player I don't always feel like I have a right to talk in the locker room.

Coach Dave Wolf enters the cramped room, decked out in black from head to toe in a Crunch polo and black slacks. He has come to Anthony Allsbury in search of black socks.

"Man, black really is slimming," says Allsbury. "You look like you lost about fifteen pounds Wolfie." Allsbury smiles, awaiting the retort as Wolf stands silent.

"Your mom sucks cock," he replies.

★ ★ ★

I am fully dressed, in uniform now, and checking myself out in the locker room mirror. I like our road uniforms best; they fit a little bit tighter than the billowy tents that serve as our home jerseys. My reverie is broken, however, when I discover that Paesens needs my shoulder pads.

"Lemme take a look at yours, Kluck," he says, pulling down the jersey material to take a look at the size of the pads.

Before I know it, I am buckling the straps of my pads onto Paesens, and it looks like I will have made the five-hour bus ride for nothing. The rest of the team files out of the locker room for warm-ups as I sit at my stall, with no shoulder pads.

I wander out into the hallway to wait for Paesens's father, whom I have never met, to bring his pads. A walk around the Marion concourse shows proof of their organizational superiority. Their apparel booths are well-stocked with team sweatshirts, T-shirts, and mugs bearing their helmet logo in green, blue, and white. Their equipment cage, adjacent to our locker room, is well stocked with extra jerseys, pants, and gear. I'm jealous. I run into Mike Powell who gives me a "what happened to you?" look.

"Your new tackle forgot his shoulder pads," I tell him, biting my tongue before I add any pleasantries about the ineptitude of the organization. At that moment I see intern Sean Lalonde rounding the corner with a set of Riddell shoulder pads in hand.

"Try these on, Kluck," he says. I yank my jersey over the hard plastic and pull them on. They fit perfectly and once again I am a football player. I jog out to join the team for warm-ups. Thank God for Sean Lalonde.

Minutes before the game, as we crowd into the cramped quarters that will serve as our bench area tonight, Anthony Allsbury is beside himself. We had somehow forgotten to say the Lord's Prayer in the locker room before the game, and, because it is part of his pregame routine, Allsbury needs to check this activity off his list. We gather hastily in the hallway adjacent to our locker rooms, and kneel, hand in hand, on the concrete.

Our father, who art in heaven . . . hallowed be thy name. Thy kingdom come, thy will be done, on earth as it is in heaven. Give us this day, our daily bread, and forgive us our trespasses, as we forgive those who trespass against us. Lead us not into temptation, but deliver us from evil. For thine is the kingdom and the power and the glory forever. Amen.

We could have been reciting Tupac lyrics or the Pledge of Allegiance for all it's worth. It is rote memorization. Football tradition like calisthenics or pain or athletic tape. I've said the prayer hundreds of times in hundreds of locker rooms all across the Midwest. I've said it more in locker rooms than I have in church. It has been led by committed Christians, atheists, and outright God-haters alike. Old football traditions die hard, and essentially, football is a game of old traditions. It is the reason for coaches denying athletes water on a hot day, or their insistence on running meaningless two-a-day practices in the heat of summer. It is because their football forefathers did it that way, and their ruddy, buzz-cut, order-barking forefathers before them. Football, kind of like Christianity, is all about dying to self. In Christianity, however, the outcome is nearness to God and the ability to enjoy Him forever, whereas in football the outcome is just pain or at best, victory.

After the prayer comes introductions, and the PA announcer for the Mayhem introduces each of us by name and number, giving all of us the opportunity to run out in front of the crowd. I have wondered how I will react to this—will I just jog slowly and give a half-hearted wave? Will I dance? Will I get at all emotionally involved and caught up in the moment? I surprise myself by doing just that— I run and bounce excitedly through my tunnel of teammates in a moment that I feel is truly beautiful. The opposing crowd boos loudly and in that moment I am happy. I wish my wife could see me doing this.

Next, the Mayhem players are introduced, and the buzz around our bench centers on one of their new rumored signees, an offensive tackle from Ohio State who weighs about 350 pounds. Watching their team introductions reminds me of where we are—a small town in the Midwest. Their guys are mostly white, many have the same buzz cuts and serious expressions that football players wore in the fifties. It looks like there are lots of families in the stands. Lots of big hair, Bud Light, and jeans shorts. These are good, Middle-American folks out for a Saturday night. I am momentarily very nostalgic for Hartford City; this whole scene reminds me of high school ball, right down to the livestock grazing next door.

I need to get over the fact that seeing us play well still surprises me. What doesn't surprise me is that Chesaurae Rhodes is a great kick returner. After an opening field goal by Marion (2–2) kicker Andy Cline gave them an early 3–0 lead, a 46-yard kickoff return by Ches puts us in position to pound the football into the end zone via an Eric Gardner run. The running game is something new this week, and after three early-season losses in which the passing game struggled, Kubiak and company are eager for ways to get the ball in their playmakers' hands.

A Ted Sauder to Jeremy Werner touchdown pass makes it 10–7, Mayhem. Werner, incidentally, is a player whose running style (stiff legged, almost Lurch-like) was mocked by our players. Nonetheless, he killed us in week two, and looks to be well on the way to killing us now. Despite all appearances, he's a top-notch indoor receiver who last played professional ball in Finland.

We answer early in the second quarter when Timmy Kubiak (who looks like a different quarterback) hits Ches with a 21-yard touchdown strike. He then comes back with a 28-yard TD strike to Richard Gills after another turnover on downs by the Mayhem. The defense, led by Allsbury, Gardner, Parker, and new CB Shaun Blackmon, is effectively shutting down the Marion offense with suffocating pass defense and a great pass rush. Gills, it should be noted because he asks me several times each day to note it, performed a Zen Buddhist cross-legged meditation in the end zone to commemorate his touchdown. There it is Rich, more to come later. For the record, Richard is not a Zen Buddhist.

The first big defensive play for the Crunch came on the next Mayhem possession. Bobby Coorlew, platooning at QB with Marion starter Sauder, threw a pick to Eric Gardner, which E.G. took 49 yards to the house.

And in what has become something of a Battle Creek Crunch tradition, the Mayhem got on the board as the half ended when Phil McDaniel hauled in a 25-yard pass from Sauder with no time left in the first half. The last twenty-five seconds of each half have proved deadly for us. It's like, as a team, we all start halftime about a minute too early.

The second half starts slowly for us as Marion continues the momentum it built at the end of the first half by stopping us on consecutive running plays at the 1-yard line and taking over possession. Though it didn't work here, the running game is proving to be key for us because as it takes pressure off of Tim Kubiak, who is playing his best game as a pro.

Funny side note: Tim Kubiak almost kills a Marion Mayhem cheerleader when he overthrows a deep bomb into their end zone that was intended for Richard Gills. The ball rockets down out of the rafters and hits this heavily made-up young lady directly on the forehead. She goes down for a few nervous minutes and the Marion training staff attends to her. After what seems like forever she gets up to the applause of thousands. Our hearts were in our throats and there wasn't a dry eye in the house. (Note: I was just kidding about it almost killing her. I was also kidding about our hearts being in our throats. More likely, we were having a good giggle about it on the sidelines.)

Another funny side note: The visitor's bench at the Marion Coliseum is located conveniently behind a seven-foot wall, meaning that in order to see any game action one has to stand on a bench. I have one of the coveted bench spots and use it to convey game information, such as down and distance, to kicker Brad Selent who spends the majority of the evening hunkered down behind the giant wall.

Marion takes advantage of its big stop, putting together a nine-play, 49-yard drive that ends with a 1-yard Sauder dive into the end zone to draw them within five at 28–23. They are unable to keep us on the ropes long, however, because Shaun Blackmon fields a short kickoff and runs it back for a score, putting us up 35–23 with thirty-nine seconds left in the third quarter.

Blackmon, a former teammate of mine with the semipro Jackson (Michigan) Bombers, has proven to be an important signee. He is also one of the most ripped individuals I have ever seen, making us all feel a little smaller by comparison.

Marion would make it interesting once more with a Sauder TD run and a fumble recovery on the ensuing drive.

Late in the game I am approached by a young kid who sidles up over to the railing that is adjacent to our bench. He has a plastic Mayhem football in his hand, and sticks his free hand out for a high five, which I gladly give. We're at the point in the game where my eyes are glued on the scoreboard clock—knowing that I'm not going to play I just want to wrap it up and get out of dodge. But as I shake the kid's hand he beams a million-dollar smile from ear to ear.

"I'm rooting for you guys now," he says. "I want you to win."

"Me too," I reply. "We need a couple of first downs," I add, "these next couple of plays are huge."

He nods somberly and we watch the game together in silence for a moment. He looks to be about eight years old and has a kind face. I hope nobody picks on him at school.

"I'll be back," he says, and scampers off to another part of the arena, returning in a few minutes with his brother who looks to be in that awkward middle-school age group. I slap the brother five and he, too, smiles from ear to ear. The two boys hunker down next to our rail to watch out the remaining moments of the game. Chesaurae Rhodes, at the other end of the bench, has caught the eye of two teenaged girls and is dancing for them, as 50 Cent's "In Da Club" thumps through the PA. Ches loves this stuff and the fans always love Ches, even on the road. Even the bus driver has gotten into the act, filling water bottles on the sideline and cheering on the team. It is one of those idyllic snapshot moments that won't last, but is really nice to experience.

"Do you play football?" I ask the younger kid.

"Not yet but I want to . . . I think we start tomorrow," he says.

"Are you nervous?"

He pauses to collect himself and ponder an answer for a moment. If he were already a football player the answer would of course be "no" because it is unacceptable to admit to anything except rock-solid confidence. I hope to myself that he doesn't get chewed up by the youth-sports megaculture in this country. A culture of intense pressure, specialization, travel teams, and psychotic parents. But then the whole city of Marion is a throwback, so maybe he has a shot at having some fun with it.

"Yeah, I'm pretty nervous," he replies.

"I always got nervous on the first day," I tell him in a moment of honesty. "Still do."

Kenny Kubiak and I are the first ones back in the postgame locker room. We enjoy the moment for a short time, alone.

"I know we don't play much," Kenny says, buoyant, "but this is still cool. There aren't many thirty-nine-year-old guys who can say they do this."

He's right. And Kubiak is one of the few who truly appreciate this experience. He is the team's loudest supporter as they're on the field, often running water bottles out to his teammates. And I think he still might be the best quarterback on the team. I appreciate Ken Kubiak's presence on the club more with each passing day because he is one of the few players with the courage to be mature and introspective.

As the rest of the players stream in, Kubiak decides that we will sign a game ball for owner Mike Powell—the same Powell who was roundly dissed on the bus ride up. The ball passes around the room and we all grab sharpies to sign. Soon Sean the Intern arrives with a case of cold beers purchased from the arena concession stand. The bottles are passed around and a toast is raised. Carmell Dennis, who played a great game at LB and DE and next to Ken Kubiak is probably the oldest guy on the team, raises his bottle of Budweiser.

He is silent for a moment before shouting out "Thundercats!" to which we reply, "Ho!"

We really are a bunch of kids.

At 11 P.M., just before boarding the bus, the autographed ball is presented to Powell, who, if I'm not mistaken, got a little misty-eyed at the whole thing. He was truly touched. "Keep it going next week," he said in true football cliché fashion. The team gathers around for one last "breakdown" on Powell before boarding the bus. L. J. Parker is off in the shadows, conversing with a woman he met in the stands. With each passing day, I am more amazed at Parker's ability to attract women.

On my way out of the arena, Coach Ashe congratulates me on a good game, and I don't have the heart to remind him that I didn't play. We also run into the cheerleader who got howitzered by Kubiak's pass. We attempt to find the bachelor Kubiak for an impromptu meeting with the girl but it never materializes. I decide to linger for a minute around the Marion equipment cage, where one of their promotional girls is straightening up for the evening. I am eyeing a tub full of green plastic Mayhem footballs, hoping to pilfer one for my son.

"Don't tell anybody," she says, handing over the football, which is probably worth about twenty-five cents to their organization. I grab a sharpie and autograph the ball for him: "To my best buddy, love, Dad." I'll stick it in his bed tonight when I get home, so that he'll wake up a see it tomorrow morning.

It's 2:00 A.M. and we are somewhere in Michigan. The bus is dark and, for a moment, quiet after our first victory. True to form, as soon as we boarded the bus the first stop was at a gas station so that the requisite cases of beer could be purchased. Several players walked to a nearby grocery store to procure hard liquor. I have never seen a group of people, collectively, who drink like this. Win or lose, happy or sad, this team is quaffing alcohol at an alarming rate.

At 2:30 A.M. I realize that we are only about forty-five minutes from home and I start to get excited about getting into my car, turning on the radio, and just being alone. I have been confined on this bus or in the tiny Marion Veterans Coliseum locker rooms with these guys for most of the weekend. No offense, but I'm ready to put them behind me. My reverie is broken, however, when we appear to be exiting the highway and pulling into a dark parking lot. I wipe away the condensation on the window and see the familiar early-morning glow of a bar sign in the distance. Stivers is the name of the place but it could be any bar anywhere. Apparently the abundance of booze on the charter bus is not sufficient for these guys. "Last call!" a boozy coach hollers from the front of the bus and about two-thirds of the guys dutifully wobble off. There are several of us in the back who are trying to sleep. Azriel Woodson, the linebacker from Detroit, simply shakes his head and mutters, "bunch of alcoholics— I don't believe this." I look back to find Herb Haygood and L. J. Parker sacked out behind blankets on the backseat of the bus. Haygood, in addition to being a world-class athlete, also appears to be the kind of guy who can sleep anywhere.

I mull my options for a moment, alone in the dark. I could continue reading or try to sleep, which to this point hasn't worked at all. On my discman, Johnny Cash is singing about how he shot a man in Reno just to watch him die. It strikes me that harder-core lyrics have never been penned. Our rap music pales in comparison to this. I look around me at Park, Haygood, and Eric Gardner all sacked out and decide that hanging around with drunks is preferable to the unreasonable two-in-the-morning anger of sitting around a bunch of guys who are successfully sleeping. I pad off the bus, climbing delicately over legs of sleeping teammates stretched across the aisle.

Stivers is your typical Midwestern watering hole. Lots of wood paneling, one of those old cigarette machines with the silver knobs, and very little else. I'm always intrigued by bars that don't really offer anything, as if to say "all you can do here is get drunk." When

I open the door and file in, I hear a cry of "Kluck!" rise up from the bar. My bleary-eyed teammates seem to become increasingly senti-mental the more hammered they get. It's always been this way, wherever I've played starting in high school. I try not to think about the fact that when we get back to Battle Creek, all of these guys will be getting into cars and driving themselves home. But hey kids, for the record, don't drink and drive and stay in school. This message brought to you by your favorite professional athlete.

There is an assortment of scantily clad (tight jeans, tight tank top), slightly chunky barmaids wiping down tables, and our team doctor Tom Martinez performing an impromptu adjustment on the neck of backup quarterback Kenny Kubiak, who is reading the paper. Kenny is always reading the paper.

I take my place at a stool between 300-pound linemen Kyle Lacksheide and new tackle/long snapper Tyler Paesens. Lacksheide eyes my Taylor Football T-shirt, worn under a track jacket with the "T" obscured. *Cops* flickers above us on the television—an appropriately depressing show for an appropriately depressing moment.

"Does that shirt say 'Gay-lor football?'" Lacksheide asks, his eyes aglow as if this new gay joke is the funniest thing he's ever heard. He is a biology education graduate of Olivet College and was a fine player at the Division III level. He has more than held his own here as well. Lacksheide is one of those guys who if you're able to converse alone with him is articulate, genuinely funny, and interesting, but in the group-think pack of the team lowers his behavior accordingly and becomes kind of an ass.

I just smile and ask the fat lineman why he isn't drinking.

"I've got a thirty-five minute drive ahead of me once we get home," he says in a rare display of self-restraint and intelligence. "I'm not going to flush four years of school down the toilet on a DUI."

I slap Lacksheide on the shoulder and tell him that he's smarter than he looks, truly proud of him, before getting up to work the room, secretly wishing these guys would just finish up so we could get out of here already.

Somebody hands me a Jack and Coke, which I halfheartedly sip. I heard once that at parties Frank Sinatra would always take drinks that were offered to him, take a sip, set it down, and then take a fresh one when they came around again. That way at the end of the night, when everyone was blotto, Frank was still fresh.

A group of just-turned-twenty-one looking girls lingers outside the bar, eyeing the bus coquettishly. They are heavily made up and kind of beefy. They look like the kind of girls who could change a tire.

"Can we come on?" they ask, no doubt serious at this hour. I tell them to ask the driver, a horny sixty-two-year-old guy named Brian who endeared himself to the team forever by filling water cups for us on the sideline during a victory that is now all but forgotten.

The contrast between what I do at home, as a father, and what I do here on the field is startling. At home I try to be a tender father to my three-year old son. We sing bedtime songs such as "Jesus Loves Me" and "Twinkle Twinkle Little Star." I serve him milk in sippy cups and read books such as the *Polar Express* for what seems like millions of times on end (but I love it). We watch *Clifford the Big Red Dog* together every morning at breakfast. "I'm T-Bone," he says, "and you're Clifford!"

Here, it's different. I run through linebacker and running back drills each day at practice and often end up filling one of the line positions in the scrimmage, locking helmets every play with men who often outweigh me by a hundred pounds.

Tonight's practice is surreal. The rain has forced us inside of a gymnasium at Olivet College that looked to be straight out of the movie *Hoosiers*. It has concrete walls surrounding the court, with bleachers above, and a stage at one end of the facility. Your classic *Happy Days* era college gymnasium. A run on balls during the last game has left us with only one football. The receivers have gotten into the habit of flipping their footballs into the stands after touchdowns (Herb Haygood) or jogging them over to the sidelines to keep (Rich Gills) à la the NFL. Unfortunately, we're not running the club on an NFL budget.

Scott Ashe, running the stretching and warm-ups tonight, is on fire. He is bemoaning the lack of rhythm on the team, as evidenced by our inability to clap together on cue in Marion, at the eight-count that follows every stretch. No clapping this week, he decides.

"We've got the only brothers in the state with no rhythm," he says. There are white guys who can get away with such statements, like Ashe, whereas the rest of us would find ourselves stuffed into the trunk of a car for saying something like that. Ashe amazes me more and more every day. Anthony Allsbury, who has begun practicing with the team as well as coaching, claps after a stretch. "And one retarded half-breed mother---er." Allsbury smiles.

It's hard not to work the word into my everyday lingo. In a football context, it is used in every possible way—as a noun, an adjective, and a verb. It means essentially nothing; it's just filler. But to my real-life friends—account executives, medical students, teachers—it wouldn't play well. I make a mental note to keep it here, on the practice field. Furthermore, Ashe seems to be the only white guy on the club who can pull it off with any sort of comfort and panache. Ashe swears like no white guy I've ever seen. Swearing, I think, is like anything else—one becomes good at it by practicing, and I just haven't practiced that much.

Tonight's practice is a good illustration of how football teams feed on the weak. Nate Adams, the radio voice of the Crunch, is on hand, and he is always a vigorous, albeit a bit awkward, participant in practice. The players take great pleasure in goofing on him behind his back as he takes one of the scout team positions in a walk-through drill. Nate is a good guy, but his fatal flaw is acting like he needs their approval. Athletes feed on that.

After a quick walk-through we run ladders, just like a high school basketball team, and are all bent over sucking wind at the end of the practice.

We gather around owner Mike Powell, who appears to have game checks, which bodes well—the team is solvent for at least one more week.

"We had some guys who missed curfew on the Rochester trip," says Powell. I know what he's going to say next—that he's going to "let it slide" this one time. I knew the curfew and the fifty-dollar-fine was meaningless. Everybody knew it.

"I'm going to let it slide this one time," says Powell, on cue, to the surprise of no one. "I felt like it was important to come together and bond as a team." That's a new angle. Notwithstanding that half of the guys we took on that trip are gone, and that we lost that game by about 30 points, I'm sure the bonding was worth it.

Kenny Kubiak leans over and taps me on the shoulder.

"Does that mean the guys that made curfew get a bonus?" he asks. Powell hands me my check, for the hefty sum of $92.37, minus taxes. It's piss-poor money, for all of the time spent and blood shed, but it's still money that makes me, for now, a pro football player.

"Don't spend it all in one place Kluck," he says, smiling. It is probably the last time I will see him smile. Mike Powell is a sinking ship.

Things Fall Apart

Chapter Eight

Game 5: Battle Creek versus Rochester

9:30 a.m. It's Mother's Day, and a Sunday, but I am once again saying good-bye to my wife and son at the door, and preparing to spend the rest of my day as a member of the Battle Creek Crunch. My wife, once again, has decided not to make the trip down for this game. She will instead be spending the afternoon with her mother, doing what normal people normally do on Mother's Day. Still, I would like her there. It's funny, all of the "you're a real pro athlete" excitement is gone from our interactions regarding the Crunch. She no longer tells me "good luck" when I leave for practice or a game. It's just the usual "what time will you be home, what should we make for dinner" type stuff. I don't expect her to be excited about this because it basically sucks for her, but in my mind's eye I envisioned her in the stands, in an officially licensed Crunch sweatshirt (Note: these don't exist.), surrounded by our friends all basking in the glow of being there to see me perform.

10:00 A.M. Halfway through the drive. Hip-hop station (bling bling and ho's doesn't feel right on a Sunday). Oldies. World music on the college station. Heavy metal (also not right on a Sunday).

10:10 A.M. Radio off.

10:40 A.M. Arrive at Kellogg Arena, park, and enter to find owner Mike Powell's wife, Karin, nailing dasher board pads to the boards around the arena. Powell himself is doing the same thing a few paces down. He looks as if he would rather be in a corner, rocking, muttering to someone to make it stop. This can't be fun for him.

Some of the players are milling around the end zone at the south side of the arena, watching Defensive Coordinator Scott Ashe tape Astroturf to the floor. The turf is still in chunks and there is a regular household vacuum cleaner sitting on about the 7-yard line. Ashe's Zen routine isn't working. He calls somebody a slapdick. I hope it isn't me.

Tim Kubiak, our starting quarterback, is already dressed in his game pants and game jersey, a full three and a half hours before kickoff. "He's in his own world today," says brother Ken. Kubiak is also sporting a brand new pair of shoes, for which he is taking a decent amount of ribbing.

10:45 A.M. We were supposed to start a walk-through at 10:45 but only half of the players are here. Kenny Kubiak looks at his watch and at the tattered field and says, "Let's start the walk-through." Nobody laughs.

"I'll move the vacuum cleaner," I reply. Again, nobody laughs.

"I'm really glad Wolf won't be here today," says Ashe of Assistant Coach Dave Wolf, who is traveling with family. "That way I'll only have Bob screaming in my ear. With Wolf it's like the parrot effect— Bob says something and then Wolf repeats it. Drives me crazy."

"It's pretty bad when you're the calmest guy on the sideline," I add.

"Yeah. But I just adapt and survive baby. Adapt and survive," he says, adding: "I want to get you in there today. Sorry again about last week."

I tell him not to worry about it, and after signing a giant birthday card for L. J. Parker's daughter Chyna (I sign it—"Happy Birthday, The Paperboy"), I make my way to the locker room to get dressed.

11:00 A.M. Three hours until game time and lunch is supposed to be here. There is no lunch. I put on my gear in a nearly empty locker room and walk down to the other end of the arena where I am to meet Rochester Raiders team photographer Bill Stiner, who is snapping some portraits of me for a potential book cover.

"It's sad when we have to line up the other team's photographer just to take pictures of us," says Parker, in the locker room.

I nod hello to a couple of the Rochester players who recognize me from the ESPN columns, and shake hands with their owner, Dave McCarthy, who is again dressed snappily in a black suit and turtleneck. McCarthy always looks like Tony Soprano.

As we are taking pictures, I ask Stiner about their travel experience and what their players are like on the road.

"Nobody drank on the bus," he says. "And nobody really went out last night, although a couple of them stayed up late playing video games."

We're in trouble.

11:30 A.M. I return to our locker room to find coach turned player Anthony Allsbury trying my helmet on newly acquired DB Brandon Brown. Brown and Allsbury played together at Western Michigan and the Crunch has failed to provide him with a helmet, shoulder pads, or a jersey for today's game, which starts in two and a half hours. Luckily, the helmet doesn't fit him, which means, for now, that I still have a helmet. Although my fear of having my uniform parceled out to new players, because the owner wasn't proactive enough to order enough stuff, may be coming true.

Players also without black (home) jerseys: Herb Haygood, Brad Selent, Anthony Allsbury.

12:00 P.M. A plate of sandwiches arrives, albeit an hour late, courtesy of team intern Sean Lalonde who is doing the work of about ten men. Lalonde's next task: track down released kicker Chuck Selinger and go to Selinger's home to collect a jersey and pair of game pants to be worn by Brad Selent. Hours until game: two.

Players still without jerseys: Allsbury, Haygood, Brown.

I sidle up to Ashe, who is telling a story to DEs Kevin Smith and Brian Wright, whom everyone thinks are related as they look almost identical. Ashe is talking about a bar fight he once had with a motorcycle gang when he was a bouncer.

"They stabbed me right in the shoulder blade," says Ashe, who is now a successful high school principal. "It was the worst pain I've ever felt, before I passed out. My philosophy as a bouncer was always to knock them out first and ask questions later, or else you'll end up getting stuck [knifed]." He adds, "I'd much rather get shot than stuck."

File that in *Conversations I Never Thought I'd Overhear*, volume one.

12:15 P.M. Trying to pretty much hide from everyone because the more I'm seen the greater the chance that I will have a part of my uniform—the helmet, jersey, whatever—taken from me and given to someone else. Call me selfish.

I end up in a supply room with Doc, who is filling water bottles for the game. We talk about how we would do things differently—sponsorships, game nights, and other issues—if we ran our own team. It's easy to be an expert in a supply closet.

"I was at the Knights [a Battle Creek minor league basketball team] game the other night and we had a table set up, but besides a couple of schedules there was nothing on the table!" says Martinez. "It's all about visibility—you need to put out banners, T-shirts, jerseys, anything with your logo to get people excited."

I ask Doc about how he has been taken care of, professionally, this season.

"I gave Mike a list of supplies that I needed at the beginning of the season, as well as a medical supply catalogue where he could get the stuff at cost," he says. "He ended up getting a few rolls of tape at a drugstore and that was basically it. In hindsight I did a few things wrong. I should have made a bigger deal out of getting left off the program, and also being referred to as the "team trainer." I also found out pretty early on that we wouldn't have an ambulance at the games because it's an extra cost . . . and we wouldn't even have one on call, for the same reason."

Gulp.

"My first game here I asked all of the staff and volunteers if any of them knew CPR, because I wanted to have a backup ready to go," he continues. "I was as nervous as the players were on opening night. I hadn't taped an ankle in six years, so I got on the Net and watched videos on how to do it, just to get myself back up to speed. And I found out the first night that I had to tape the Port Huron guys as well as our guys . . . talk about an ungrateful group of people. But it ended up that I became the only league doctor who traveled everywhere with his team."

12:20 P.M. I am interrupted by someone shouting my name. It's Allsbury.

"See ya Doc," I say, "I have to go give up my jersey."

"Kluck, I need your helmet logos," says Allsbury, frantic. "I can't have Brandon Brown, starting FS, All-Mid American Conference, out there without logos."

I trudge into the Crunch office where Allsbury is already peeling the logos off. He shakes his head. Brown is trying on helmets in the same room, trying to find one that will fit as the minutes click away toward game time. Brown finally finds the right fit, and ends up wearing a helmet that belongs to quarterback Tim Kubiak. Brown smiles, revealing the fact that all of his front teeth are capped in gold. Nice. I just lost my helmet to Flava Flav.

"This is unbelievable," Allsbury says. "F—kin' stupid."

This expression, (pronounced *faw-kin stow-pid*), is one of the team's favorite Allsbury-isms and it is frequently mimicked. The good news is that Brown now has a helmet that fits. His gold teeth gleam from behind the metal bars. He still has no jersey.

12:22 P.M. In the locker room I discover that CB Shaun Blackmon's last game check bounced. He is irate, and ready to storm Mike Powell's office to talk about it. Shaun Blackmon's name is added to an increasingly growing list of people I wouldn't want mad at me. He's huge.

"Let it wait till after the game," says Eric Gardner who is sitting up against the cinder-block wall with his iPod headphones in ear and eyes closed. "Don't let it be a distraction right now."

Blackmon, momentarily, is appeased. I look at Gardner and we both shake our heads. I ask Gardner, arguably our best player, if he has been approached about moving up—possibly to the AFL or Canada. Gardner is leading the league in TDs and has proven himself on offense, defense, and special teams.

"I've had a few people say things, but people are always saying shit," he says.

I couldn't have said it better myself.

12:30 P.M. The coaches call the special teamers and skill players out onto the field for warm-ups. Only a few of us leave the locker room.

"We only have two footballs," says WR Richard Gills. "You can't do much with two footballs. I'll go out when I'm ready to go out."

Gills is an enigma—sometimes the happy-go-lucky team guy, sometimes surly. He is a physical specimen at 6 feet, 4 inches, and 225 pounds but thus far his numbers haven't reflected his physical ability. He has, though, scored in the last two games and his end-zone celebrations have become something of an attraction. After the first score he laid on his side like a Victorian model and posed for pictures. Last week, he crossed his legs in the end zone and meditated. Gills spent several weeks up with the AFL's Grand Rapids Rampage earlier this season, and I ask him if he saw a discernible difference in competition.

"It's a lot easier down here," he says quickly. "There are a lot more defenses in the AFL. More schemes. And the game is faster."

"I have a new end-zone dance for you," he adds, before I go. "And I want a personal ESPN interview on end-zone dances." I'm not exactly sure if he's kidding but I tell him I will work on it.

I go out onto the field minus helmet logos (they were replaced by gooey strips of adhesive along the side of my black helmet), to snap a few to holder Kenny Kubiak. We have only two footballs—one for the quarterbacks to throw to receivers, one for the kicker/snapper/holder. Welcome to the big time.

I run into Lalonde on my way off the field. He has produced another shipment of game balls.

Taking a few moments before a game to reflect in the stands—
where I probably should have stayed.

From left, line coach Anthony Allsbury, head coach Bob Kubiak, and defensive coordinator Scott Ashe. This is perhaps the last time they would all be smiling.

"Adapt and survive baby." Scott Ashe is either meditating or thinking of ways to cut off the author's testicles.

Linebacker L. J. Parker, who would go on to sign with the AFL's Grand Rapids Rampage.

The pre-game breakdown, in the bowels of Kellogg Arena. From left, Ken Kubiak (14), Tom Mack, Brian Dolph (8), Kyle Lacksheide (bald), and "The Preacher" Azriel Woodson (9).

*Our most explosive,
and enigmatic,
player—WR/DB
Eric Gardner in
pre-game warmups.*

*Eric Gardner (left), who learned everything he knows about
scoring touchdowns from the author (right).*

The author as defensive end, pass rushing in mop-up action vs. the New York/New Jersey Revolution.

Two long snappers—the author, with Joe Bock, age 46, of the New York/New Jersey Revolution. Bock played in the NFL, USFL, and AFL.

The quintessential Jersey guy, Anthony DeFalco of the New York/New Jersey Revolution—he played without shoulder pads.

Kenny Kubiak leads the Crunch's offensive charge. Note the empty stands.

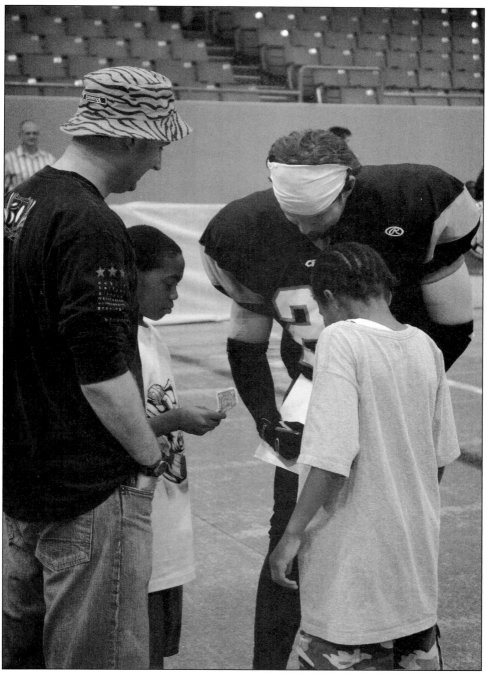

Signing autographs was one of this season's sublime pleasures. That's my buddy Regner in the ridiculous hat, and my dad looking on from a distance.

The "EXIT" sign—a metaphor for this experience, or just the quickest way to our cars? I thought about that sign a lot this season.

"There's a girl back there pumping them up as we speak," he says, hopefully. He shakes his head. I thank him for his hard work, noticing that he has begun to win over the affections of the other players who now realize that without him there probably wouldn't be a team.

1:00 P.M. One hour before kickoff. The team is assembled in the locker room with the coaches who are trying to make sure that each player has a jersey and a helmet for the game—any concerns about matching player numbers to position or program listing are long forgotten. I volunteer to give my jersey to Herb Haygood because the coaches realize that his home jersey, number 27, is probably hanging on a wall in Don Lonsway's home, and Lonsway lives in Kalamazoo. The team didn't bother to collect jerseys after the first couple of games and the players who were released just kept them.

Haygood seems genuinely touched that I would give up my jersey for him and it brings the beginnings of a smile to his usually expressionless face. Haygood reacts to the chaos around him with stoicism, as opposed to talk or worry. He spent the minutes before game time signing trading cards for teammates. "Just do my number justice," I tell him jokingly. Several of the players clap in recognition of my sacrifice for the team. The truth is, I had no choice. Star WR takes precedence over talentless writer. Haygood begins the task of taping up the jersey to fit. For reasons known only by Mike Powell, he ordered size XXL jerseys for every player on the team. They fit like tents on even the large guys.

Next, Kenny Kubiak is forced to give up his number 14 for new DB Brandon Brown. Bob Kubiak produces a faded black practice jersey bearing the number 44, which Kenny slips over his pads. It looks ridiculous and everybody knows it.

"Mean Machine! Mean Machine!" he shouts, in reference to Burt Reynolds's ragtag bunch in the football classic *The Longest Yard*. Kenny is trying to put a positive spin on things, but I know he is embarrassed.

Finally, a jersey arrives for Anthony Allsbury, who has been pacing the locker room like a caged animal. He will be wearing the number 6 because it was collected from the home of Carmell Dennis, who lives near the arena. Dennis is not active for today's game. Allsbury is less than thrilled.

"I'm sorry about this," says Bob Kubiak, who I know feels terrible. "I called Mike at least a dozen times this week to remind him about jerseys and helmets."

"It's not your responsibility," I tell him.

"Well," he says, "more fodder for the book," adding, "I ran semi-pro teams that were more organized than this. When I coached at that level I collected all of the jerseys and pants after the game and if you didn't have a uniform at your locker for the next game, you didn't play. Simple as that."

The team files out for pregame warm-ups and I am left alone, sitting at my stall in game pants, game shoes, gloves, and an Under Armour shirt.

1:05 P.M. The team is out for warm-ups and I am alone in the locker room. I think for a few minutes about what to do. My options are: Wear one of Kubiak's ratty practice jerseys over my pads and still, technically, "dress" for the game. Not happening. I'm too vain. Another option is to remain in my football pants and wait for the possibility of another jersey to arrive. Not bad, but where would I wait? By myself here? On the sidelines? I finally decide to peel off the pants, Under Armour, and gloves and put on my "street clothes" or "civvies."

I use the moment of quiet to fish my cell phone out of my bag and call my dad. As always, he is there for a word of encouragement. I run down my litany of gripes and he is appropriately shocked at the bush-league nature of our team. We talk about how, in a football sense, I have a dark cloud over my head—how every organization I've really ever been a part of as a football player has been garbage. As is usually the case with these calls, I begin to self-counsel myself by the end of the call.

"I'm just going to relax and treat this as a last hurrah," I hear myself telling him.

"You never really had a first hurrah," he says.

Nice.

1:55 P.M. I slip into my as-yet-unstolen white number 25 Crunch jersey and join the team on the sidelines, in street clothes. There are no more than five hundred people in the stands, and there were no introductions, no lights, and no smoke machine today. I also become jealous when I realize that the Illegal Motion dance team, which boasts about twenty dancers, has three complete changes of uniform and matching sweatshirts. They are by far the most professional part of this organization.

"You're on the IR now," jokes Selent, trying to make the most of an awkward situation.

"Yeah, his pride is injured," says Lacksheide, who gets this week's award for stating the obvious.

"Thanks Lacksheide," I reply. "Appreciate the encouragement."

The players are shouting at each other on the sideline, the usual pregame aggressive banter that happens between players, and is directed at the opposing team.

"Let's go get 'em," shouts one of our DB's, "Let's tap that ass! Let's show 'em who's boss!" I'm struck by how overtly aggressive and sexual this talk has become, which makes the inevitable headlines in the newspaper, the headlines that come every season about your favorite athlete assaulting a wife, girlfriend, or acquaintance, that much less surprising. The unbridled rage and aggression of a football team is pretty remarkable.

For the first time I notice that Delano Harry, the defensive back from Wayne State who had a cup of coffee with the Rampage, has not dressed for the game. This is the same Harry who provided some stability to our defensive backfield and played a great game at CB in our win over Marion. I am perplexed. Why we would tinker with the lineup now— essentially cutting Harry to sign Brandon Brown—is confusing to me.

I stop thinking about Delano long enough to realize that we are about to start the game but haven't yet had the national anthem. The officials seem to notice this as well, and Nate Adams, our radio guy, ambles out from behind the boards to sing. Adams does a serviceable job with the song—not great, but I've heard much worse.

The Raiders (4–1), who led the league in total offense entering the game, waste no time in taking advantage of our distractions, scoring on their first play from scrimmage as receiver Maurice Jackson slips behind the Crunch secondary and grabs a 36-yard touchdown from quarterback Matt Cottengim. Cottengim seems to stand about 7 feet tall and has the perpetual tan and chiseled features of a male model. Chalk this up to another reason to hate him. He replaced starting quarterback Omar Baker, lost for the majority of the season with a badly broken jaw, before our first game and has proceeded to lead the league in passing and touchdown passes. He is a product of East Stroudsburg University (Pennsylvania) and along with Noah Fehrenbach and Jackson has ignited the league's most potent offense. While Baker was more of a scrambler, Cottengim is a classic drop-back quarterback.

"He'll tell you where he's going with his eyes," says Ashe before the game. "From the minute he comes up to the line of scrimmage he's looking right at the guy who's getting the ball."

This may be true but we still couldn't stop him.

The duo was far from finished as Jackson caught four more touchdowns on the day, while Cottengim was nearly flawless after some early struggles, recording the five touchdowns to Jackson with just one interception. Jackson was a four-year letterman at Syracuse University and spent time with the NFL's Buffalo Bills as well as the BC Lions of the CFL.

Rochester has equal success on the ground as running back Reggie Cox dashes through our defense on draw plays, designed to exploit hard-charging defensive ends who rush upfield. The undersized Cox, a University of Buffalo product, exploits our middle for 84 yards on 15 carries with three touchdowns. Cottengim plays the game virtually untouched on pass attempts as the Battle Creek defensive rush is noticeably absent.

The pass rush disappeared because Crunch defensive line coach turned DE Anthony Allsbury disappeared with a high ankle sprain. Allsbury had almost single-handedly infused the team with a pass rush that had been absent for the first two games. He displayed a variety of moves and speed around the corner, in addition to a cadre of lame-but-endearing sack dances, including "the worm." Our defense missed him tonight. He came to the bench writhing in pain and whipped off his size XXL helmet, made to fit over one of the largest heads I have ever seen. Allsbury almost looks like an alien on the field, with a giant head bobbling on top of a normal-sized body.

Sometime around the second quarter I wander out to the concourse to call my wife and spread some of the sunshine I'm experiencing her way. Having already unloaded on my dad, I just tell her what happened in a dull monotone, and tell her how much I can't wait to get home to her. Out of the corner of my eye I see a familiar figure in a Crunch jersey approach me in the concourse; it is former practice player Jacob Hoxie. He looks to have embroidered his own last name onto the back of his black number 46 jersey. Hoxie was one of our most dedicated practice attendees but has yet to suit up in a game. I had seen Hoxie prowling the arena earlier, sitting angrily by himself in an empty corner of the stands adjacent to our bench. It was an almost cinematic gesture.

"They came up to me before the game trying to get my jersey," he says, "I told them where they could go. I earned this jersey. I built this field."

Hoxie is belligerent and upset over his lack of playing time. He looks slightly boozed up too but I would stop short of making this statement definitively, because I like Hoxie and what would it prove? It's been a tough season for Hoxie, and he's someone whom I've felt sympathy for from time to time. He tried to endear himself to teammates with tough talk and swagger but it ended up backfiring on him because they simply made him a target. "I'm moving to Florida," he says. "Taking my construction business down there to start over. How in the world can they not activate a guy who runs a 4.3 [second] 40 [yard dash]?"

I hear myself telling him not to let bitterness take root, and to just chalk the season up to experience. A shot taken. A chance to do things most people couldn't or wouldn't. This is just minutes after my own internal tantrum over losing my jersey for the night. I should take my own advice once in a while.

Despite the Raider offense basically scoring at will, Eric Gardner is almost single-handedly keeping us in the football game. Gardner's 36-yard kickoff return for a touchdown gave the Crunch some life after Rochester's opening score, and we tied the game at 20 with a Kubiak-to-Gardner strike on the opening drive of the second half.

Gardner adds a 12-yard fumble return for a TD with 1:27 left in the third quarter that pulls us within seven points at 34–27. Although Rochester is more talented and better prepared, we're actually hanging with them.

We show signs of life in the second half, with long completions to Richard Gills and Gardner, but interceptions on consecutive drives in the second half led to two Cottengim-to-Jackson strikes and killed our momentum from Gardner's fumble return. We also get a couple of injury scares in the second half as L. J. Parker and Chesaurae Rhodes both go down awkwardly on the Home Depot–purchased black Astroturf that was haphazardly taped over the ends of our end zones. Parker flings his helmet to the concrete floor in disgust, the noise of plastic on concrete rattling through the empty arena.

"It's a knee," says Doc Martinez, after a cursory sideline examination. In the NFL, the player would be wheeled through a tunnel directly to an exam room with an MRI machine and an X-ray. This being a far cry from the NFL though, it is probably more realistic to think that this is the last medical exam that Parker will have on the knee. Rhodes injured his back slipping on a piece of the same turf, which came unfixed from the concrete beneath it. I find

Parker in the locker room before I go, and give him a hug. I let him know I'll be praying for him, and that there's a lot more football left for him, after this. Although I'm not sure how much even I believe that.

Herb Haygood, brought in for his NFL cache and big-play ability, was held to 5 receptions for 40 yards. Tim Kubiak finished 15-for-28 for 167 yards and the lone TD to Gardner. I feel for him again, as the "you're just the quarterback because your brother is the coach" rumors are bound to swirl again this week.

"I think we'll make some minor adjustments but we just need to start doing what we do and doing it better," said Bob Kubiak to the *Battle Creek Enquirer*. Kubiak, like most coaches who have been in the game for any amount of time, has mastered the delicate art of talking to the media for a long time but not saying anything. "We need to make sure that all the coaches and players are on the same page and know their own roles."

Rochester was dominant on both sides of the ball, defeating the Crunch, 61–27. The stands were basically empty.

To say that the scattered nature of last week's pregame has caused some soul-searching would be a massive understatement. Not so much soul-searching, I guess, but wondering if when I show up at practice next week there will still be a team there to meet me.

I get a cryptic e-mail from Mike Powell, which basically says that "I'm looking for investors or financing" to get the team through the rest of the season. It is the last I will probably hear from him.

I decide today, before practice, to ring Jeff Spitaleri from the league office to get his take on the status of the Crunch.

"What have you heard?" he asks, when I get him on the phone. Spitaleri, like the rest of the league founders, is a friendly guy who probably loves football more than he loves doing business, but has a pretty sound mind for both. He sounds harried. I can tell he is reticent to spill the whole truth to the writer but he presses on anyway.

"I got an e-mail from him a week or so ago basically saying that he was tapped out, that he was all out of money, and open to suggestions," says Spitaleri. "I sat on it for a few days because, quite frankly, I didn't want to e-mail him when I was upset.

"Powell never paid his franchise fees [twenty-five thousand dollars] or his league dues [several thousand per week]," says Spitaleri. "He had several people from the community—one of whom was Bob Kubiak—approach him before the season and offer to partner but he basically turned them all away."

The picture he is painting of Powell is different, certainly, than the one I encountered at the beginning of the project—that of a guy full of hope and excitement, who assured me that Battle Creek would be a model franchise.

"I think Powell basically figured that he would start a team and open the doors and then people would show up," Spitaleri continues, "but it doesn't work that way. He hasn't done the marketing. Apparently he took in anywhere from thirty-five to fifty thousand dollars in sponsorship money . . . and I want to know where that money is. I mean, he only paid a thousand dollars for the dasher board pads and hasn't paid for the turf or anything yet. Where's the rest of the money?"

I tell Spitaleri that there has been very little marketing to speak of—none of the usual player appearances at malls, etc.—and the few things we have done (a golf tournament, the bowling alley) have been abject failures that feature the players standing around chatting with each other and the one or two fans who have bothered to show.

"I heard you had to give up your jersey last week," he adds. Word, apparently, travels fast. I ask him if there are any alternative ownership groups moving to the forefront.

"Bob Kubiak is still interested," he says. "At this point I'm basically giving it away. If you can come in and fix this franchise then it's yours."

I learn, though, that Spitaleri and his staff are dealing with additional problems. There is the problem of traveling the Crunch to

Lehigh Valley for this weekend's game to the tune of about six to seven thousand dollars when it's all said and done. And then the prospect of bringing the NY/NJ Revolution, the GLIFL's all-travel club, into town for two home games in June—a cost that is borne entirely by the home club.

"To complicate things," he says, "the Revolution only want to fly now. They're tired of bussing. The Outlawz have offered free use of their bus, which basically amounts to a long, custom RV with twenty-four seats, but NY/NJ wants to fly now. I even offered to waive Lehigh Valley's league dues for four months, in exchange for the bus. But NY/NJ thinks the Outlawz bus is unsafe. But this is a bus league. What do they think this is, the NFL?"

Spitaleri raises my spirits momentarily when he mentions something about Tom Martinez possibly taking over the ownership reigns. I am excited for us, but worried for the Doc—with young children and a fiancée this nightmare is the last thing he needs; it appears to be ingredient A in the recipe for ruining one's life (see Mike Powell).

"Also, Kubiak is going to talk to all of you guys tonight about taking pay cuts at practice," he says. "I just wanted to give you the heads-up."

I leave the stressed Spitaleri to attend to the rest of his business, ending the call with more questions than answers.

I have mixed feelings driving to practice tonight. On one hand, I am just excited to put the pads on and be a football player again, after not playing at all in the last game. Practices have become my games, at least for now.

I arrive about forty minutes early in hopes of getting a lift in the Olivet College weight room, which is one of the only perks on which the Crunch staff has actually delivered. The weight room is empty and unlocked, and the house stereo is tuned to heavy metal. *Ahh*. Life, for now, is good. I slip into my own world with the weights—bench presses, hang cleans, lat pulls, leg extensions. It feels good to be physical again and reminds me of my college weight room experiences.

My reverie is broken, however, when the players start to arrive. Many, I find, haven't been paid since week three.

"I haven't gotten a paycheck since the second game," says Bob Kubiak, who has joined me in the weight room. "My wife is pissed off at me . . . she had vacations and stuff planned . . . had basically already spent the money."

I ask Kubiak about his own designs on the ownership.

"I just want to finish this thing out," he says. "If it was the beginning of the season and we could really market the team and do things right, I would be completely interested. But it's tough now, midseason. But you know what? I've always been an underdog. We're underdogs every year at Olivet and I like that." Kubiak agrees to sit down with me at some point and talk about this at length, but he leaves the weight room as quickly as he entered. There are, no doubt, problems to be solved elsewhere.

I finish my workout, relatively high on the good lift, and dress for the walk out to the practice field. I encounter Carmell Dennis and Delano Harry, neither of whom dressed for the last game, on my way out. Neither are happy.

"If it ain't broke, don't fix it," says Harry. "We should have stayed with the lineup we had for the Marion game."

"Who did they cut you for?" asks Dennis.

"Some lineman," says Harry.

It was Kevin Kramer, I tell him, a kid who dressed but didn't play a down in the game.

"I can see bringing a guy in once in a while, but to bring in a guy who's never even practiced, that's semipro stuff," he says.

The Dennis decision was odd as well. He played well in the Marion game, often providing a pass rush from each of the d-line positions.

"I can see if you bring somebody in and he kicks my ass, that's fine," he says. "Find somebody that can come in here and put me on my back. But through training camp and half the year I haven't seen a linebacker here who's better than me."

Down on the field there is more discontent, with Chesaurae Rhodes leading the charge. Ches, like most of the players, hasn't received a game check in quite some time.

"Where he live?" Ches asks, of Powell. "'Cause I'll go there and get the money myself!"

Somebody suggests that Powell will probably be at practice. (He won't.)

"If he comes, he better come with a police escort," says Ches, "because I'll take it out of his skull."

I am reminded that there are players here who truly count on these paychecks. More important, guys like Ches count on this as a way to get film and get noticed by scouts from bigger leagues such as the AFL, CFL, or NFL Europe. Slowly, I think, they are seeing that dream slip away.

Numbers are down tonight. As we line up to stretch there seem to be only a handful of us here. I look around at the mismatched helmets and jerseys. We really are a ragtag bunch.

"What are there, like eight of you here tonight?" says Doc. "You might get some PT."

L. J. Parker limps to the field in street clothes. He tore up his knee in the last game against Rochester but has been unable to get a needed MRI because he doesn't have health insurance. Parker works as a cook and a bouncer at a bar. And the workmen's compensation coverage we were supposed to receive is no good because Powell allegedly failed to pay in the required amount to cover the team.

"I've got a van," says Lacksheide, "let's go find him and get our paychecks." Lacksheide is pursuing the dream in his own way, having attended a Scout Camp Regional Combine in Chicago over the weekend where he was put through the usual battery of tests, in addition to one-on-one drills.

"I was the only D-III guy there," he says, "there were linemen from Ohio State and a bunch of other big schools. I did twenty-eight reps on the bench but they took two of them away. I was pissed."

Lacksheide is one of the few players on the Crunch with the size and tools to move up. He is, even at 310 pounds, one of our best-conditioned athletes and frequently wins our postpractice conditioning sprints and gassers.

Not surprisingly, practice is lackluster. I am excited, however; with the low numbers, I get a shot at playing Jack Linebacker with the starting defense, often lining up in man coverage against our starting WRs. I am beginning to feel comfortable again, playing the LB/FS hybrid position. I glide back into my pass drops, eyes scanning the field to pick up my receiver and cover the deep portion of the field. I notice the different approaches of each of our receivers. Eric Gardner always seems to glide, makes everything look easy, and, staying true to ghetto fashion, has to pull up his shorts (which have fallen around his ass) after every play. Brian Dolph looks me right in the eye coming off the snap, and uses his eyes to fool me into committing to a move that he often won't make. This is especially humiliating. Ches is workmanlike and keeps his eyes down while running each of his routes.

I am, by my own admission, having a great practice. I snag footballs out of the air in the warm-up receiving drills, and almost intercept Kenny Kubiak in the scrimmage to the surprise of almost everyone. On one of the last plays, I run stride for stride with Ches, on a nine-route, which is a fly pattern straight up the sideline. When running like this, in man coverage, the world ceases to exist; all I hear is my breathing, Ches's breathing, and the thuddy footfalls of shoes against artificial turf. I can tell he is getting the ball because he speeds up his pattern a bit and his eyes widen as the ball approaches. I throw up my arms as the ball careens toward him, and deflect his attention enough that he drops the football. A cheer goes up from the defense as Ches drops to the ground for ten pushups, his custom after every drop.

"Nice coverage, Ted," he says on our way back to the huddle.

"You're a bad man, Teddy, looking like a loose-hipped defensive back out there!" shouts Coach Ashe. I really couldn't feel much better.

"Where you playing this summer, Ted?" asks backup LB and long-time semipro player Dewaynne Thompson as we walk off the field. His question means that he is interested in recruiting me to play wherever he plays, which means he thinks I can play football. For the first time in a long time I feel like a football player.

"Hang around," says Coach Kubiak to the team, "we're going to have a quick meeting to talk frankly about some things."

As is customary, we clump together for a breakdown in the end zone.

"Let's go 'Mike' on three!" says Ches, to a round of nervous laughter. Mike has always been the object of the players' scorn, but never more than tonight. For his sake, and for his safety, I hope he never shows his face again because some of these guys are truly nuts.

To say that the atmosphere in the meeting is somber would be an understatement. Many of us think this may have been our last practice. We sit in a drab white meeting room, on folding chairs, flipping through Olivet College media guides. It has the feel of a giant doctor's office with all of us nervous to hear the news that is to come. The team, in a very real sense, is on life support right now.

Finally, Kubiak enters. He recounts the tales of Powell failing to pay league dues, and about the coaches not being paid since week two. His words are met with silence, but the players are shaking their heads and many, it seems, are chomping at the bit to talk.

"I wouldn't expect to get paid, by Powell, for the rest of the season," Kubiak says. "I wouldn't blame any of you for getting up and walking out of here, and if you do there will be no hard feelings." He pauses for a moment, to look around the room. "But the coaches and I are committed to finishing this thing out. We've got some options . . ."

He goes on to explain a scenario wherein if we make the playoffs, all of the playoff dollars allocated to the team would be split amongst the players. The playoffs though, at this point, seem to be a pipe dream.

"As I see it," he says, "this thing has three parts. Part A is just getting down to Lehigh Valley and playing that game . . . getting through this week. Part B is finishing out the rest of the season, and Part C is fixing this thing, and doing our marketing so that we can make next year a success. That's the easy part."

"I've never been 1–4 in my life and I don't plan on staying 1–4," adds Ashe. "I just finished telling my kids about sticking things out and never giving up . . . so how would it look if we gave up now?" The players nod their agreement. Shockingly, this coach-talk-never-give-up-rah stuff is getting to them. "So I think we should cowboy up and go down there and take care of business. But I need commitments from you guys, and I need to know that we're not going down there to get our asses tapped."

Kubiak asks for a show of hands. A "who's in?" sort of question. Several hands go up. Finally, Azriel Woodson, the quiet but scathing linebacker who has played in indoor leagues before, speaks up.

"I played for a team in South Dakota a couple of years ago that didn't pay the players for five weeks," he says. "Let me ask you guys a question. Most of you would be playing semipro ball this summer anyway, right? You all would be putting your bodies on the line for free. You guys know that ain't nobody moving up from semipro, but at least with this you can get some film . . . and maybe get the chance to move up. I'm in. But I want to say that I saw this coming for a long time."

I am shocked. I thought that Woodson would be one of the first to walk out. He actually ended up being a quiet, eloquent voice of reason. I look around the room and find the players in various states of reaction. Ken and Tim Kubiak saw this coming and have been informed by their brother throughout. Tim Kubiak, like usual, just chews sunflower seeds and spits the husks impassively into a cup. Anthony Allsbury looks exhausted and has the look of "what have I gotten myself into?" written all over his face. He removes his gigantic NY Yankees ball cap and rubs his gigantic bald head. Parker looks sullen and can only shake his head. He asks me, in a whisper, what he should do about his knee and I have no answers for him. Herb

Haygood, a quiet pragmatist, looks neither dismayed nor hopeful, but suggests the occasional marketing idea. Haygood, I've learned, has already parlayed his name and connection with Kubiak into a coaching gig at Olivet College next season.

Finally, Kubiak explains the dilemma of health insurance and the fact that Powell effectively screwed the players out of health coverage by telling the players that they would be covered, and then failing to make the necessary payments into workman's comp. I look around the room at the majority of my teammates who either work hourly jobs or have no jobs at all. Ches gets up out of his seat and stands silently for a moment. He goes first to Ashe and Allsbury to shake their hands, and finally makes his way to Kubiak at the front of the room. "I'm out fellas," is all he says. And just like that, Chesaurae Rhodes, fan favorite, is out the door.

Kubiak stands silently for a moment before motioning to intern Sean Lalonde.

"Go get his helmet and jersey," he says. "We're going to need them on Saturday."

After the meeting breaks up the players stand around for a long time in the parking lot, nobody really wanting to go home. Ches, it turns out, wouldn't give up his helmet without getting his release papers—papers which, I'm guessing, don't even exist. We've never seen copies of our contracts so to think that actual release papers exist in a file somewhere is a stretch. I think Ches is free to pursue other teams given the fact that he hasn't been paid and the fact that nobody (Powell, Kubiak) has the time or resources to pursue legal action against him. Contracts, I'm finding, mean very little at this level.

"What do you think of all this, Kluck?" says Woodson as we walk to our cars.

"I agree with what you said in the meeting," I tell him. I was impressed by his logic in there. But I still, fundamentally, have a problem with these guys putting their bodies through hell on ridiculously thin turf, without the dignity of even receiving a paycheck to cover their gas money. I have half a mind to tell L. J. Parker, my friend, to walk away now and cut his losses. I seriously consider doing so.

"I know a girl who has worked for professional indoor teams in marketing before, who could have really helped Powell out," says Woodson. "But he said he wasn't interested, that he had it covered."

Wednesday, 6:45 P.M. I am fifteen minutes early for practice and find Herb Haygood and Eric Gardner in the weight room when I arrive. I have been looking forward to this workout all day. The shaky status of the team has me a little depressed during the day, and it is all I can do to drag myself off the couch to write and shoot e-mails to other teams, trying to make contingency plans should the Crunch decide to go belly-up.

From: "Ted Kluck"
To: Manchester Titans
Subject: American Author, ESPN
Date: Thu, 25 May 2006 16:19:27 -0400
Dear Manchester Titans,

I am a frequent contributor to ESPN.com Page 2 and author of "Facing Tyson: 15 Fighters, 15 Stories" to be released worldwide in October by the Lyons Press (www.lyonspress.com).

I am also currently playing a season of professional indoor football as chronicled in a series of columns on ESPN.com Page 2 (see www.glifl.com for the entire lineup). The material I'm collecting will be used in my second book with Lyons, to be called "Tackling Walter Mitty: A Season Inside Professional Football."

I have included the most recent columns below:
http://sports.espn.go.com/espn/page2/story?page=kluck/051214
http://sports.espn.go.com/espn/page2/story?page=kluck/060411

That said, my current club (the Battle Creek Crunch) looks to be on the verge of folding, and I thought that a pro experience overseas might add an interesting angle to the book. I would envision a week or so of practicing with your club, and perhaps working into a series or two in an upcoming game. I play FB/LB and longsnap, and am 6'2" 215 lbs with American collegiate and semipro experience.

Drop me a note if you're interested in the idea or feel free to contact me with any questions.

Best,
Ted Kluck

I approach Gardner and Haygood, and give them both the standard athlete hug (half handshake, half high five, chest bump, two solid whacks on the back). They are discussing the weekend's trip.

"I think they should just fold it up," says Gardner. It is as outspoken a statement as I have heard him make all season.

"We got a lot of our best players out," he continues. "Parker is hurt, Allsbury is hurt, and Gills got suspended for four games for pushing a ref."

I make my way around the weight room, going about my business alone while rap music throbs through the facility. The Olivet College weight room is much like any other weight room I've ever been in—it smells faintly of sweat and antiseptic, and the walls are littered with motivational sayings such as "Olivet College Football— on a collision course with the MIAA title!" and "Did anyone outwork you today?" Oddly, as a writer, even on days where I am super productive and crank out twenty pages or so, I feel like I've done very little work, which is why football is so satisfying right now. Football is a very modern game—it's black and white, there is a winner and loser in every game and on almost every play. And in a postmodern world of never ending "dialogue" and relativism, this is a comfort to me.

I try to be thankful for the workout I'm getting, right here, right now, rather than feeling anxious about this weekend. Although, as we get closer to 7 P.M., none of the players are showing up. Harry Pettaway pulls up but leaves his Ford Escape running in the parking lot. Pettaway is wearing his usual suit and tie—I think, at some level, he relishes the role of the white-collar athlete and is often heard discussing business ideas. Through the darkness of a long bus ride, he once fired up his laptop and showed me photos of the land he owns in Northern Michigan. He works the room, sharing the latest rumors regarding the future of the Crunch.

Anthony Allsbury enters the weight room wearing a pair of shorts, a polo shirt, and golf spikes bearing fresh grass stains. He walks immediately over to a bar with what looks to be upwards of 225 pounds loaded on. The players stop what they're doing and casually glance in his direction. Allsbury has the demeanor of someone who used to be the "king of the weight room" and I sense that the guys want to see if he still has it. He picks up the bar and cleans it toward his chest, however, he begins to wobble and the plates loudly crash off of either side of the bar. Allsbury looks around self-consciously before letting out an embarrassed laugh.

7:10 p.m. It has become rather obvious that there will be no practice this evening. Our workouts done, we have sprawled out on the carpet in the Olivet Football complex lobby, awaiting a word of direction from an increasingly stressed Bob Kubiak. There are only a few of us left—Haygood, Gardner, me, Pettaway, Lacksheide, Tim Kubiak, and Tyler Paesens. Timmy has shown up in jeans and is sitting on the only sofa, munching sunflower seeds.

7:12 P.M. "This is stupid," declares Tim, his first words of the evening, before getting up and walking out. Gardner, head bobbing to his omnipresent iPod, follows suit.

7:14 P.M. "Where's Tim?" asks Bob Kubiak.

"He left," replies Haygood, "and he looked a little hot." Kubiak leaves, ostensibly to retrieve his brother from the parking lot.

"I think we should open up a strip bar," Pettaway suggests to Haygood. The team is obsessed with strip bars, with any number of players, at any time, scheming about opening a place of their own.

"I ran one once," offers one of the coaches, "used the money to pay for my master's program. That was a two-to-three-million-dollar-per-year operation for us back in the day. There were whores working out of the back, we loaned money, we ran numbers. It was easy money back then, there for the taking. We had two Detroit cops working the door for us, so that part of things was taken care of.

"But I remember one night," he continues, "I got in an argument with a guy over a hundred bucks, and I wound up in the parking lot with a gun pointed at the back of my head. I had a one-year-old son at the time and thought about what it would be like for him to grow up without a father. It put things in perspective for me."

I nod at him in agreement, father to father, as I know the feeling that he's describing. I often feel the same way about doing this.

7:25 P.M. Kubiak returns, without his brother, to bring us up to speed on where things stand. We are short on players and uniforms, but the Lehigh Valley Outlawz and owner Jim DePaul have agreed to cover our travel for the trip. Now, it seems, it is just a matter of finding players.

"I'll play both ways," says Lacksheide, "let's just find seven guys and go down there and kick some ass!"

Lacksheide is a meathead. Nobody says anything, except to laugh at the seven guys comment. I feel that we could sign Peyton Manning and Ray Lewis this week and still not beat Lehigh Valley. I think folding the tent would probably be the most courageous thing to do but I am not naive enough to think it will happen. This ship will go down, and it will go down in an ugly way.

"We're leaving at 10 P.M. on Friday," says Kubiak. "We'll drive straight through the night, get day rooms for a little rest on Saturday, play the game, and then take the bus home right after the game is over. If we win this game fellas, there's a good chance we make the playoffs and then the playoff money, about seventy-five hundred dollars, is ours to split among the players. It's going to be hard to go down there and win . . . I mean, I'm not saying it's going to be hard . . . but it's going to be difficult."

Huh?

"I got a call from Ches today," says Kubiak, changing the subject. He pronounces Ches like "Shez." He sounds like a maître d' at a French bistro. "He apologized for walking out and said he wants to play. He told me Mike Powell is paying him out of his own personal salary."

The players voice their displeasure at one of their own brokering a side deal (albeit one that will probably never happen) with the owner.

But for now, the prodigal son returns. Maybe.

Good Story

Chapter Nine

> He's a complicated man, no one understands
> him but his woman.
>
> —Isaac Hayes, Theme from *Shaft*

A football season is a living thing, in that yesterday's darkness often gives way to today's dawn. Yet, as I drive my wife and son through rain which started in Lansing and has continued through the Ohio turnpike, through the entire state of Pennsylvania, and into our shabby hotel parking lot, all I am seeing is darkness. A long drive to suit up (if we have enough uniforms) for a game that I probably won't play in, and a game that we will probably lose by an embarrassing margin.

The trip, with them, has been a pleasure though. I am thankful for the fact that my wife and I can drive twelve hours together and not only not be annoyed with each other by the end, but really enjoy every minute. We enjoyed the luxury of being able to start and end conversations, while at home we are so busy that everything seems clipped.

I am also amazed at how understanding she is of the football, and all of the neurotic tics that come with it. To be a football wife is to be a part-time shrink. In one sentence she hears me talk about how I love the camaraderie, how there is nothing like it. In the next, she hears me talk about how sometimes I feel like an outsider on my own team, how I'm not like the rest of my teammates and how I've always been that way. She'll hear me talk about how badly I want to play in this game, but then how fearful I am about playing badly or, truthfully, getting hurt. When I was a kid playing football I felt like I had nothing to lose—like I couldn't imagine a life without football. But now there is a beautiful wife, a beautiful son that I love, and the ability to do something I love (writing) for a living. Every play feels like roulette and I have less room in my life for a broken leg, a separated shoulder or, God forbid, something worse.

I tell her, somewhere in Pennsylvania (I'm amazed at how relatively unpopulated this state is—between Pittsburgh and Philly there's basically nothing), how crazy it is that this happened at all. I remember last year, watching the NFL draft, deciding to send some e-mails around to see if I could set something up. The draft (my buddy Chris Regner and I call it Draftmas and wear the jerseys of our favorite busts), for me, is the high point on the football calendar and the time of year when I want to play football the most. I love the hype, I love the magazines, I love reading the scouting reports. Yes, I am a dork. I scour through the heights and weights and the player descriptions, still measuring myself against the young guys on the pages. If I had a scouting report, it might read something like this:

Ted Kluck, FB/LB
Height: 6' 2"
Weight: 215
Age: 30
Strengths: Tall
Weaknesses: A little stiff in the hips. Doesn't run well. Has trouble flipping his hips. Cut high. Tends to disappear in big games. Used to love the game but now not so sure. Saw a copy of Pride and Prejudice *in his locker which makes me think he's soft. Would rather be a cat than a dog. Spends a little too much time in coffee shops.*

After ten years of marriage there are no secrets with her. She knew, watching Draftmas last year, that I wanted to play again and she knows now that I am scared—scared of playing because I have reached a level of football where nearly everyone is bigger, faster, and stronger than I am; but scared of not playing at the same time, because playing is how I used to define myself. I have become, in football scouting terms, a head case.

"Football doesn't define you," she tells me, for what seems like the millionth time.

Neither, apparently, does money, or the ability to provide well for my family. When I wheel into our hotel at 10:30 P.M. on Friday night, my heart sinks. The place is a dump. We have been rooked. We upgraded to a "suite," which is actually just a larger version of the shabby guest room, with a sofa and a couple of crappy chairs thrown in. The "award-winning Belgian Waffle Bar" I read about in the brochure is a standard kitchen toaster and a package of frozen waffles. I have my sleeping son (he's especially beautiful when he's sleeping) slung over my shoulder and get him tucked into bed before launching into a profanity-laced tirade about the room and about how stupid all of this is. I smell pot smoke and hear the sounds of ghetto kids racing up and down the hallway outside our room. Through the paper-thin walls I think I actually hear my neighbor's thoughts. It will take my wife hours to calm me down. I thank her for loving me, and for being loyal to me, though sometimes I wonder why she does.

Unable to sleep, I fire up my laptop and receive the following e-mail:

Dear Ted,

I'm a big fan of ESPN the Magazine and of the site, especially Page 2. The internet is the best way for us Brits to stay informed about our favourite sport, as over here there is only ever some rushed together coverage around the Superbowl that tends to focus on the amount of potato chips consumed by the American domestic television audience or the cost of a 30 second advertising slot at halftime . . .

You would be most welcome to come over and spend time with the Titans, we're only 1 game into our season and our last game isn't until August 20th. We also have some charity fundraising events coming up and are close enough geographically to a lot of other British teams so you could meet them as well. Our coaching staff has been involved in the sport in the UK since it began 20 years ago (this season is "Britbowl XX") and will be able to give you any info you need or interesting anecdotes. I'm sure there wouldn't be a problem with you playing in one or more games for us as well.

The key point I need to make though is that the teams in the British American Football League are not professional. In fact only NFL Europe teams are pro in the whole of Europe. I hope this doesn't present an obstacle, we'd love to have you come over. Our team is made up of a diverse range of people; we have police officers, paramedics, business professionals and tax avoiding students (when they can be bothered to get out of bed that is).

I hope to hear from you,

Best Regards,

James Tresman
Linebacker, Head of Media, Sales Consultant, Bears fan!

Game 6: Battle Creek vs. Lehigh Valley

The hours leading up to the game on Saturday are a blur. I spend the majority of the morning attempting (unsuccessfully) to book us into a different hotel for the night, and after a nervous lunch, make the drive out to Bethlehem, Pennsylvania, and Stabler Arena with wife and son in tow. I had read descriptions of Bethlehem as the quintessential hard, blue-collar steel town and it certainly lives up to those accounts. One thinks of the word *bleak*. We spend nearly an hour driving through Bethlehem, up and down hills on sad, narrow streets, looking for a coffee shop in which to kill a few minutes and find none. What we see are block after block of ramshackle apartment buildings, each with a DirectTV dish hanging off its porch like mushrooms springing forth after a hard rain. After yesterday's drive and the litany of failures that followed it, I am in no frame of mind to play a football game. L. J. Parker calls to ask why I didn't make the trip on the bus, and to make sure I'm dressing for the game. The fact that somebody on the team is thinking of me improves my mood considerably.

"It was Parker," I tell my wife. "Calling to see where I'm at." She rolls her eyes. She is beginning to get nervous about four hours at a strange, hostile arena chasing Tristan around by herself and, combined with the bleak steel-town surroundings, I can see her mood darken with each passing minute.

We wheel our car into the arena, which is on the campus of Lehigh University. Today there is a women's lacrosse tournament in session, so the campus is teeming with minivans and families.

"I'm with the arena football people," I tell one of the polo-clad college girls manning some sort of registration table on the drive in. She looks at me like I'm crazy. I read the logo on her polo which says "USA Women's Lacrosse." She and her partner both have the ruddy but radiant look college girls get when they're in the sun too long. Gulp.

"So that's what's going on!" they say, breathily, before asking me a few questions about the game. "We had a bus come through here earlier."

"That girl was flirting with you," my wife informs me as we pull away. Oh man. Here we go. It's going to be a long evening.

We find a spot and make our way to the players' entrance at the back of the arena, past the TV trucks. It's cool to be one of the performers, going in through the secret back entrance. I think of this almost everywhere we play and it never ceases to bring a smile to my face. My wife, however, is relatively disgusted. Upon entering the arena we are hit with a tsunamic wave of posturing and testosterone. There is hip-hop. There are players strutting around in Under Armour, looking tough. Lehigh's trashy dance squad (their version of Illegal Motion) is gyrating on the turf. While I slap hands with teammates and coaches, I can see Kristin getting more and more freaked out by the whole thing. She is mentally retreating to a happy place—a place that doesn't include football or her husband. I give Tris a quick tour of the field and walk them back out to the car.

"I hate jock culture," she says before praying with me and kissing me goodbye for the next four hours. "I don't know why you're doing this."

"I don't either," I reply. "But it's almost over."

I trudge back down to the players' entrance, relatively deflated. As I walk toward the door it is blocked by a middle-aged man in a Lehigh Valley Outlawz T-shirt.

"I'm a Crunch player," I tell him, my exhausted eyes never leaving the dirty concrete under my feet.

"How do I know that?" he says, flashing me some stereotypical East Coast attitude, mixed with security-guard fake moxie. "You got some team ID?"

We don't even have paychecks. We barely have jerseys, helmets, or an owner. How does this little walkie-talkie–clutching chump expect me to produce team ID? The fact that they spell Outlawz with a "z" (like so many nail salons and tanning bed places) at the end makes me almost murderously angry at this moment.

"No ID," I tell him. "Ask somebody in there." I momentarily consider jumping back in the car and driving twelve hours back to Lansing, just cutting my losses.

"Go on in," he says, real security apparently much less important than the appearance of security. The first face I see upon entering the arena is Doc Martinez. I'm glad he made the trip. He usually provides calm in the midst of these storms.

Inside I am briefed by Doc on the news of the last two days, the most significant of which involves Powell, who apparently went to the hospital with a heart attack. There was speculation, right up until the time of the bus trip, that he was going to show up. The arena tunnels are furious with activity—dancers running in and out of their locker rooms, and players from both teams running out to inspect the turf, which looks brand-new. I run into Sean Lalonde to ask him a question about Kristin's tickets. I introduce him to my wife as "the intern" on a cell phone call, but he corrects me.

"I'm actually the GM now," he says. "I was promoted yesterday."

I have seen Lalonde's stock rise amongst the team. Whereas he was earlier seen as the object of scorn, he now has almost universal respect in the locker room because the players see the kind of effort he puts forth. I am genuinely happy for him.

The arena itself is impressive, seating about five thousand, with Outlawz logos at midfield and in the two end zones. I wander up to the wall with my son, when another Outlawz security thug in a T-shirt says "you can't go on the field." These guys are great—it's like the Pentagon in here.

I enter the crowded locker room (still the nicest we've dressed in thus far) to find that the league has supplied helmet decals for us, so that each helmet has identical logos. Like kids at Christmas, we peel the heavy vinyl logos off a sheet and place them on our helmets.

"It's the least we could do," says GLIFL co-commissioner Jeff Spitaleri. "Last week was embarrassing."

I also see Richard Gills, the big WR who was supposedly suspended by the league for four games but has miraculously reappeared.

"Gills!" I shout. "I thought you were suspended . . . or incarcerated!"

This gets a laugh from the guys as Gills just shakes his head. At any rate, he's a good kid and I'm glad to have him back. As if on cue, he asks me when he's going to get his personal interview. At least his priorities are in order.

As the players dress—many still complaining about Powell, the bus trip, and no paychecks—Azriel Woodson begins to speak about the importance of focusing on today's game.

"We're like the league's bastard children," he says. "We ain't getting nothing from our parents so the league has to step in and meet our needs. We ain't got no logos, we ain't got no money . . . no food."

The room hums its approval. The Preacher is on a roll.

"All we can do is win. Ain't nobody respecting us . . . we gotta take their respect!" *Mmm hmm.* "There's only one place to go fellas. One way! And that's down."

The room stops for a moment, as the momentum of the pregame sermon is lost. I tap Aze on the shoulder pads.

"You mean up, Aze."

"Yeah, up. I meant there's only one way to go and that's up!"

The team cracks up and his speech has the unintentional good effect of loosening us up. I refer to Aze as Knute Rockne for the rest of the afternoon—my first attempt at joking with the surly LB.

On the field we have one of our most crisp warm-up sessions of the season. I work with the defensive line, going through the pass rush drills—rip move, swim move, and the rest—and playing defensive end in the pregame scrimmage. I even snap well, which is satisfying on a personal level—each ball spiraling directly back into the holder's hands—but I find out shortly before kickoff that backup QB Kenny Kubiak will be doing the snapping tonight.

"For the record, I think you should be snapping," says Martinez, who always has a kind word. I wish I could agree with him but Kubiak is just more consistent.

I sidle up to Chesaurae Rhodes who is relaxing along the boards. Ches has rejoined the team but has seemed a little distant—miffed, I think, at being snubbed for one of the starting CB positions earlier today when Ashe announced the starters. Ashe instead went with a big lineup of Herb Haygood and Shaun Blackmon, each of whom measure over 6 feet.

"Glad to see you back, man," I offer. Ches has always been one of my favorite players but has seen much of his boyish enthusiasm sapped by the hard season.

"Yeah, I had a lot of guys calling me last week asking me to come back," he says.

"I called you last week," I tell him, "but not to ask you to come back. I just wanted to wish you well. You have to do what you have to do."

★ ★ ★

Bob Kubiak has never struck me as a pregame speech kind of guy. Usually he gives the garden variety "let's limit our mistakes and play aggressively" kind of speech. The last week has been emotional for him. In addition to finding enough players and uniforms to make the trip, I learned that he has also inquired into team ownership himself. He looks tired as he approaches us just minutes before game time, seated on concrete steps underneath the arena bleachers.

"I can sense that you guys are a little down," he says. Kubiak is your classic football coach and has the same rough charisma that all of the good ones have. Even when he's pissed off at you, you can't help but like the guy. "You might be down because of the paychecks or the bus ride or whatever," he continues. "But I want you to forget about all of that. The next two hours are all you really have at this point. The next two hours are your salvation."

It was an amazing pep talk, short and succinct, and as Dickie Dunn says in *Slapshot* (how many times can I reasonably quote Dickie Dunn in this book without it becoming a problem?), he really captured the spirit of the thing. The atmosphere is charged in Stabler Arena, and we are introduced to a chorus of boos, which is great. And after the Outlawz PA announcer (one of the worst I've ever heard, with a "Bueller . . . Bueller" type monotone that comes off like fingernails on a chalkboard) introduces every single Outlawz player, coach, water boy, trainer, masseuse, bus driver, and dancer; we start the game at what seems like an hour later. The Outlawz are taking the game lightly, I can tell. They even have a WR who calls himself Superman and wears a red cape out onto the field during introductions. What a clown.

"Hey Smitty," I say to 260-pound DE Kevin Smith as Superman jiggles through his introduction dance. "Do me a favor and kill that guy."

Once the smoke clears, however, we jump on them with an early safety courtesy of one Kevin Smith.

Early in the game I realize I have my first heckler of the season. I have been turning around periodically to check on my wife and son, who have seats about ten rows above the Crunch bench, a perfect vantage point for me to turn around and see their beautiful faces now and then. Soon, I begin hearing my name called, and not by a woman's voice. I turn around and see an older-looking gentleman gawking at me and smiling dumbly, and a younger fat guy in his mid-thirties with a crew cut and a ruddy face that seems to get ruddier with each beer he drinks tonight. It is the younger guy, I discern, doing the name yelling. He seems to take great pleasure in just yelling my name, and when I turn around he sits there with a dumb look on his face as though he doesn't know what to say next. Finally, I walk over to where our bench comes closest to where they're seated, after they call my name. This seems to disarm them a bit; I have clearly broken the heckler/athlete barrier. I wonder if they want to have a conversation? I have posted a couple of messages on the GLIFL message board for fans; perhaps these guys post there as well. They ask what position I play and I tell them. They ask me why I'm not getting into the game and I shrug my shoulders. It's all very intelligent stuff. I turn and walk back to the bench and they will continue to shout my name periodically for the rest of the night.

Although Smitty and the defense get things started, Crunch quarterback Tim Kubiak is stellar, going 13-for-25 for 165 yards and three touchdowns. He also runs for a score. It is something of a coming-out party for the embattled quarterback, as I had I hoped. This performance will finally silence the nepotism critics. Timmy finally looks comfortable back there, and it shows. His comfort is thanks in no small part to Kyle Lacksheide and Harry Pettaway on our offensive line, who effectively nullify a much-hyped Outlawz pass rush, including a white guy with a flattop named Ramos who calls himself "Hollywood."

Eric Gardner is sensational as well, leading B.C.'s rushing attack with 15 carries for 48 yards and two touchdowns. He also hauls in three catches for 39 yards and two touchdowns. Gardner's first touchdown catch is on a post corner, and he hauls in the ball mere inches away from the brick wall that juts out of the end zone at Stabler Arena.

A finally healthy Brian Dolph catches seven balls for 70 yards, including a sweet one-handed stab, while Rich Gills catches 4 for 45.

A kick returner named Mark Barionette keeps Lehigh Valley in the contest throughout. His efforts routinely give the Outlawz starting position in our territory, resulting in scoring runs by Outlawz quarterback Chad Schwenk and running back Steve Cook. We even go so far as to dig out the rule book at halftime, looking into the ramifications of Brad Selent just booming the ball out of bounds rather than kick to the shifty Barionette.

The game is iced when Herb Haygood intercepts a Chad Schwenk pass and returns it 24 yards to the house. This is a Haygood that hasn't played defense since high school, but started and finished the game at cornerback. He celebrates in the end zone by flipping the ball to the referee without incident. Herb Haygood dances for nobody.

We improved to 2–4 in the GLIFL with the 59–53 win.

Walking toward the locker room after the game I catch the eye of an exhausted-looking Bob Kubiak standing alone in the concourse.

"You did it, man, you kept this thing together," I tell him as we embrace. "Congratulations."

It's as close to emotional as I've seen Kubiak all year. He's exhausted, after single-handedly putting a team together and making this trip, this win, happen.

"This was supposed to be relaxing for me," he says. "It was supposed to be the time where I just coached and made a few extra bucks and didn't worry about stuff. Now I've got to go straight from this right into coaching at Olivet."

Like all good coaches he has trouble enjoying the moment, instead worrying about the future. He is kind and friendly to my wife and son who have met me in the concourse. And, after offering them a sandwich, promises to get me into the game next week.

Ken Kubiak is bounding around the locker room like a child. It's as buoyant and demonstrative as I've ever seen him. He seems to have found his niche as a long snapper and played very well tonight. He peels off his number 14 road jersey and tosses it into a pile as the other players continue to pour into the locker room after milling around on the field for the postgame prayer, a semi-pro tradition.

"You sticking around, Teddy? Sticking around to have a beer or something?" Before I can answer he bounces into another room and comes back with two footballs. "Sign these," he says.

"Who are they for?" I ask.

"It's a surprise," he says, adding, "Allsbury's mom has a surprise for us on the bus!"

Laughter throughout. Kyle Lacksheide enters the room, to find an on-fire Kubiak.

"Hey look, it's Mr. Holding!" he says to Lacksheide, who was flagged for successive holding calls near the end of the game. "Thanks to you we're getting out of here an hour later!"

Ken Kubiak is the new Dave Wolf.

— —*Original Message*— —
From: Ted Kluck
To: Mike Powell
Sent: Tuesday, May 30, 2006 7:26 PM
Subject: Health

Hey Mike,

Heard you had some health issues over the weekend . . . just writing to see how you're doing and wish you a speedy recovery. Hope all is well.

Best,
Ted

Ted—

I guess maybe a little age catching up with me as well as a little stress getting to my heart. At any rate, I am turning ownership of the team over to the league, for health reasons. It's wearing me down, and Friday night was the eye-opener. Nobody else other than Sean, Karin and I seem to want to make the true commitment to the overall operations of the team. I am sapped physically and financially myself.

Welcome to the world of minor league sports! I at least tried to make it happen.

—Mike

After a few more e-mails of this nature, I am shocked when Powell agrees to meet with me in Battle Creek. I meet him on an unseasonably warm late-May day, at a place called the Automotive Mile on Dickman Road where there are no fewer than ten car dealerships lined up side by side. For the last few weeks Powell has been working full-time as a salesman at Henkel Mazda and, in his last e-mail, says "we can walk around the lot and talk, pretend like you're interested in buying a car." This will, no doubt, be the first interview I've conducted in which I've pretended to be buying a car.

When I wheel my car into the lot I see Powell in his black Crunch pullover, finishing up a deal with a couple of eager new-car buyers. I wait in my car until he finishes up with them, and then walk out to greet him.

"There you are again, looking like a writer," he says, in reference to my long hair and glasses. Powell likes giving me a hard time about my look. He is friendly though, as always, and it is good to break the ice and get past the tension. We begin walking out toward the rows of fresh new cars, and for all anyone knows I am an eager young buyer. I even open the door of a little sports coupe and smell the new car smell wafting out, just to complete the charade.

"That's actually a 2005," he says. "If you're interested we're pricing those to sell." I thought we were pretending. "Selling cars is a little bit more fun than doing insurance and investments. Here the product is tangible . . . it's fun to take the customers for test drives and stuff, rather than just saying 'let's put a couple thousand dollars in a mutual fund and see how it performs.'"

I begin by asking Powell if he has any regrets about owning the Crunch.

"Absolutely none," he says, without pause. I am a little surprised, guessing that based on what he's been through physically and financially he would have second thoughts. I know I would.

"I got this thing started," he says, "and I think it still has the potential to be a positive thing here in the community. I was talking to my son the other day, telling him that in a few days, after the league takes over, I will no longer be owner of the Battle Creek Crunch. But he said 'you'll always be the founder.' And that's cool. I hadn't looked at it that way."

Powell already has the car salesman's sunburn on his balding head. And, as with those presidential photo montages showing the toll the office takes on presidents, I feel that Powell, forty-five, has aged decades over the last year.

"Karin [his wife] and I basically came to a point where we realized I can't do this anymore, physically or financially," he says. "My credit cards are maxed out. I don't think anybody realizes how much of our own money we put into this. Probably about sixty thousand or seventy thousand dollars when it's all said and done. And I had a lot of people say that they were going to help me and then, for various reasons good and bad, not do much. It's basically been Sean, Karin and me running the show for a long time."

I feel the need to make Powell feel better, largely because in spite of his mistakes, I like the guy. This whole thing is about people taking a last shot, I tell him. It's that way with the players, too. Lots of us have regrets.

"I think we underestimated a little bit, what it would take," he continues. "A lot of our sponsorship sales were in trades and a lot of the sponsors haven't actually paid their cash. That, with the bad attendance the first three games, really sunk us financially." He pauses, collecting his thoughts. "I really don't know what more we could have done though."

I mention the sensitive topic of player paychecks, aware that he is aware of the fact that guys haven't been paid in weeks. I ask him if the players have been contacting him about their money.

"We've had a few guys call—guys like Smitty, Wright, and Blackmon who I knew from the Jackson Bombers. They were counting on this money and, if I'm able to sell the team, I have every intention of paying every player for every game he played," he says. "But I tell you, Chesaurae Rhodes is about to drive me to drink. He calls me five or six times a day."

Five or six times a day?

"Minimum. Sometimes more like eight or nine. He calls me ranting about his money, about how he made this a priority and he's counting on it. I told him starting out that he really shouldn't make it a priority. Chesaurae Rhodes is not going to make his living playing pro football. None of these guys are. These guys all need to have regular jobs or backup plans . . . school or something," he says. "I like Ches. I love the energy he brings to the game but I don't think he has much in the way of financial sense."

I find this hard to believe about Ches, in a way. I also find it interesting that despite our many differences, my loyalty, as a teammate, is with Ches.

We spend a few minutes chatting about the team, and about our resurgence of late. Powell expresses how tough it's been for him to stay quiet on personnel issues so as not to step on Kubiak's toes, especially when the team was struggling. Apparently, at the height of Tim Kubiak's struggles, the team was considering signing former MSU star and NFL journeyman Ryan Van Dyke, but we both commented on Tim Kubiak's coming-of-age performance against Lehigh Valley. I am reminded of how much Powell truly loves the game and how much he cares. He is, in spite of everything else, still our biggest fan. I ask him about his health issues.

"I was rushed to the hospital on Friday night," he says. "Everybody talks about pain in your left side when you have a heart attack . . . for me it was shortness of breath and it felt like my heart was pounding out of my chest. I couldn't catch my breath for about thirty minutes."

"I had an EKG this morning and will have an MRI later in the week," he says. "They're trying to determine exactly what it is I'm dealing with. But they have me on all kinds of meds now—a nitro patch, some blood pressure pills . . . I feel like I'm swimming sometimes . . . like I'm not all there."

I ask Powell if he will be at the game on Saturday, and he answered in the affirmative. I choose not to dwell on the awkwardness that that might cause among the players and coaches. He promises to bring me the T-shirts and sweatshirts I ordered, that he forgot today. I know that I will never see them.

"But that Lehigh Valley game was something else . . . it was a classic," he says. "The webcast didn't work but I sat there in the recliner, under all the blankets and stuff, just updating the live scoreboard on the Web site—just hitting refresh, refresh. My wife kept threatening to take away the laptop . . . because I'm sure my blood pressure was going up."

Game 7: Battle Creek versus NY/NJ

Where does one begin writing about a night that was nearly perfect? Do I start with the car ride down with my dad, having him there with me through the walk-throughs and the time leading up to the game, so that he could see me doing all of the cool behind-the-scenes-writer stuff, coupled with all of the cool behind-the-scenes-athlete stuff that might make dads proud?

Do I start with a conversation I had with Kevin Hanratty, the quarterback for a team, the Revolution, that doesn't have a home arena and travels to all of its games? Hanratty is a winsome kid (looks just like Ralph Macchio from the old Karate Kid movies) with a thick New York accent, who tells me in said accent that he put off a year of law school to do this—to travel hundreds of hours by bus to get beat every week (the Revs are currently 0–6) and get paid only a hundred bucks a game (the standard Revolution player contract.)

"You gotta play next year!" he tells me, in no uncertain terms. I share with him the beating he would take from my wife if she heard him say that. I think I am maritally obligated to never play anywhere again, for the rest of my life. "How old are you?" he asks.

"Thirty," I respond.

"You're just a kid," Hanratty (who truly is just a kid) says. "There's nothing like playing," he says. "You can't go to the park and say, 'Hey do you guys want to find an arena and run around for two hours and get smacked into some boards?' You can only do this once."

He is joined by an Italian teammate, Ad DeFalco, who looks as though he could bench press Buicks. If it were possible for a man to be all chest and arms, it would be this side of beef. He echoes Hanratty's sentiments and wishes us luck tonight. I remark on how classy these guys are for having just ridden a bus for ten hours.

"That guy, DeFalco, looks like the quintessential Jersey guy," my dad remarks. "It's like you cross the state line and you're presented with millions of tough-looking guys with slicked-back hair and rolled-up shirtsleeves."

As the minutes tick away before kickoff, I feel perfectly at ease for the first time all season. I have my dad with me on the bench and we are simply watching the experience go by. The Illegal Motion dancers are warming up on the field, the players are milling around, and I am warming to the idea that I may actually get real game experience tonight on defense if we blow these guys out. Herb Haygood, in particular, has been lobbying for me to the coaches. I enjoy showing the players to my dad, and introducing them all by name. It means something to me that these guys like me and don't just tolerate my presence. I am learning, in some small way, to be one of them. I've mimicked their hugs, their handshakes, and their mannerisms now to the point where our interactions are clean and easy. I fast-forward in my mind for a moment to how much I will miss them when this is all over. As the dancers float by and the music booms, I realize, in a Cameron Croweish mix tape kind of moment, how lucky we all are to be here, together, right now.

L. J. Parker drops onto the bench next to my dad and me, and I get a brief update on his family situation. He is working the door at a bar now, still watching the kids most of every day. He and his girl-friend still aren't getting along, though she has threatened to pro-pose to him at the last game. That could get complicated, I tell him, wishing I had some better advice for him. I look at the bulky knee brace on his right knee and say a little prayer that he doesn't get hurt, which is something I do for him before almost every game. Parker still doesn't have health insurance coverage.

I have a similar pregame relationship conversation with Doc Martinez, who left two tickets at will call for his girlfriend as a sort of ultimatum: Show up and we'll keep working on the relationship and sort things out. Don't show up and it's over. The Doc looks tired and I can tell the situation with his girlfriend, the demands of his job, and the potential for being involved in one of the ownership groups taking over the Crunch is taking its toll on him.

I relatively float through warm-ups, feeling loose and lively as the rock and roll music throbs over the PA and I run through drills with the defensive line. We work the rip move, the swim move, and form tackling. I can see my dad, just over the wall, munching con-tentedly on a piece of pizza. My friends Chris and Beth Regner have just settled into their seats above our bench. Chris has purchased a tiger-print Crunch hat at the souvenir stand and he looks ridiculous. All is right with the world just now. Allsbury is imploring his charges on the defensive line to pitch a shutout, and blow these guys out. "Let's get Kluck in there!" he shouts, before we break down. What he doesn't know is that I very much want to get in there. I finally, for the first time in years, feel comfortable on a football field.

After player introductions (smoke, spotlights, and the rest—I could get used to this) we jump on top with a quick Tim Kubiak post-corner to a wide-open Eric Gardner on the first play from scrimmage.

I congratulate Timmy on his way off the field and turn to Doc, who is scanning the crowd for signs of his girl, to no avail. He looks crestfallen.

"It's her loss, Doc," I tell him. It is all I can think of to say. I am buoyant when it looks like we are going to indeed hand a beating to the Revolution, which would pave the way for playing time for me. I see Hanratty running for his life, pursued by Anthony Allsbury and Harry Pettaway. I see a Revs offense that is struggling to find any sort of rhythm.

We get the ball back and quickly move down the field again, ending the drive on an Eric Gardner halfback option pass to Brian Dolph, who for the second-straight week has been unbelievably impressive. Dolph literally picks this wobbly football out of the hands of the defensive back and lopes into the end zone untouched. His only celebratory move is a point in the direction of his wife and toddler son, who sit in the same seats for every game.

"Dolph seems a little different," said my dad after meeting him before the game. "Not to take anything away from the other guys, but there's something classy about him."

I agree. It's good to have Dolph back for a lot of reasons. He has established himself as our chain-mover—the guy who keeps drives alive on third down by going up for footballs and often crashing into the boards.

The other story line of the first half has been the play of our kicker, Brad Selent, who in the first half made three tackles on kickoffs and had to run the football on a botched extra-point snap (thankfully, not mine—I've already gotten one kicker almost killed this season). I see him grabbing a handful of aspirin from the Doc, and rubbing copious amounts of a mystery solution he keeps in a small vial on his sore legs and back. He is hobbling along the sideline, attempting to keep his legs loose, but flexes his skinny kicker guns at his wife and kids in the stands, just to let them know he's okay.

Offensively, the Revolution is struggling to mount any kind of an attack. They are most effective when running the football—their pass plays involve Hanratty either running for his life or launching the ball into the stands to avoid a sack. They look tired and sluggish, like a team who travels many hours by bus each week.

The coaches have to try to be stern at halftime. They come in and give us the usual football jargon—don't let up, it's a 0–0 game in the second half, blah, blah, blah. But we know we own these guys and it's just a matter of finishing it out.

"We've got to get some performance out of the kickoff team!" Kubiak shouts, genuinely pissed. Our kickoff team has been an Achilles' heel all season, typically giving the opposing team great field position, which puts additional pressure on our defense. "Nobody takes a blow on kickoffs! It's a third of the game!"

My knees are jiggling with excitement, sensing that this blowout could give me my first taste of significant action since week two. Kyle Lacksheide, who has stripped off his jersey and pads during the break, has other things on his mind:

"Hand me a slice of that pizza," he says. "I'm hungry."

"You're fat," says his linemate at Olivet College Tyler Paesens. Together they have accounted for much of our success the last couple of weeks. Neither would be called a physical specimen at first glance—both are pale mammoths over 300 pounds—but on the field they are surprisingly quick and destructive.

"Your balls stink," Lacksheide retorts, the two men bantering back and forth across me. They spend the majority of their time together—living in the same ramshackle Olivet College off-campus apartment, and working together at TP's Bar. Suddenly the talk turns to my book.

"Hey Kluck, what are you going to put on the cover?" Paesens asks. I know that he is setting me up for something, so I just sit quietly, waiting for the comment to arrive. "Because I think you should just use a big picture of my junk," he suggests, gesturing toward his crotchal region.

"If I had your junk I wouldn't put it on the cover of a book," I reply, pretty pleased with myself. I am turning into an adolescent.

Paesens laughs and I help him attach the buckles on his shoulder pads as we begin to ready ourselves for the second half.

"You know, I always kind of feel like a gladiator when I do this," he says. "You can't run around and punch people for two hours in real life."

Lacksheide reaches for a slice of the pepperoni and mushroom Hungry Howie's pizza that has been sitting on a training table since several hours before the game.

"I need some whiskey, too," he adds. "Timmy, you got any Jack Daniels in your bag?"

Kubiak just smiles. He has played two straight weeks of great football and will finish this game with four more touchdowns and no picks. He has approached the last several weeks with a quiet seriousness that was absent before. He is, now, a pro quarterback.

"Just have Coach Wolf breathe on you," I tell Lacksheide. This gets a laugh from L. J. Parker who has been sitting silently, with a towel over his head.

As we head out the door for the second half, Herb Haygood looks in my direction and mouths the words "be ready."

"Be ready to play some d-end this half," says Coach Ashe on the sidelines. I immediately wrench the shiny black helmet, off since pregame warm-ups, over my head and buckle the chinstrap. I stretch my quads and calves, leaning on the boards.

Unfortunately the Revs show some signs of life in the second half, after replacing the injured Hanratty with backup QB Karim McFarlane, who can barely see over the line of scrimmage but is much more mobile and slippery than his counterpart. McFarlane's mad jail-break scrambles result in a couple of third-quarter scores for the Revs, and I pace nervously, watching my playing time slip away. Just in case, I keep a close but nonannoying distance in relationship to Scott Ashe, so that he sees that if needed I will be ready.

After another quick Eric Gardner score, I get the signal from Ashe. "You're in at nose this series." I have no time to be nervous.

Harry Pettaway and Lacksheide are already approaching me on the sideline to give some advice.

"Use your quicks on that center," says Pettaway.

"Take a little jab step to your right and then go left on him," says Lacksheide, suggesting a move that I ran on him during warm-ups.

I am surprisingly relaxed as I jog out onto the field to join my teammates. Tom Mack, the big TE/DE who was released earlier in the season but re-signed for this game settles in next to me at the right defensive end spot. It's good to see T-Mack again. I take a quick look over my left shoulder and locate my wife and family in the stands, to make sure that they know I'm in.

McFarlane settles in under the center, a round-looking black guy who wears a dark visor over his eyes. I am surprised to find that he is several inches shorter than I am, but he probably still outweighs me by at least 50 pounds. It will be important to not let him into my body, otherwise it will be all over for me. I need to quickly make a move and commit. I am alarmed by the sense of quiet at the line of scrimmage. There is no trash talk, just the sound of breathing. I can feel the prickles of the worn, bright-green Astroturf under my fingers. It feels good to be a football player again.

At the snap I make a quick jab step to my right and rush left with a swim move, just as Lacksheide suggested. Shockingly, I blow right past the center and for a moment have McFarlane squarely in my sights. Visions of a sack and my name immortalized on the stat sheet dance through my head until I feel a heavy hand grabbing at the back of my shoulder pads. The center is hanging on for dear life, risking a holding call rather than giving up an embarrassing sack. His grip gives McFarlane enough time to slither away and fire a strike downfield. As we trail the play, he turns to me and says, "Good rush." After a few more plays, with the Revs threatening, I am replaced by Harry Pettaway. The players, Kenny Kubiak and Herb Haygood in particular, offer their congratulations as I come off the field. I look up in the stands and get a thumbs-up from my wife and my dad. I pace to the end of the bench where Scott Ashe is barking instructions at the rest of the defensive line. This is all very familiar and I like it.

At the end of the quarter the Illegal Motion dancers flood the bench area, getting ready to perform. They are trying to talk to Doc's son, Chance, age 7, who fills the water bottles for the team. They say things like "he's so cute" and try to muss up his hair. He is terrified of them. I am terrified of them as well. There's something dangerous about dancers in spandex.

"He's my wingman," says the Doc, rallying a bit after the disappointment of his girl not showing. After three quarters she's still absent.

The Revs are mounting an offensive attack leaning on their ground game and the running of Matt Holmes. After tasting my first action I am hungry for more. I'm more animated cheering on my team than I've been the entire season.

"You're in at defensive end," says Ashe, "not this series but the next." I keep one eye on the action and one eye on the clock, as we move the football down the field and finally score, on a great run by Chesaurae Rhodes who for the first time all season has gotten reps at running back. The elusive but strong Ches is a natural back there and bulls the pile for the last 6 yards into the end zone.

"Can you run down under a kick for me?" asks the wild-eyed Coach Wolf, who has returned to work with the special teams. Special teams are the most dangerous aspect of football, and being on the kickoff team is akin to being a kamikaze bomber. It's something I've wanted to try all season. I thought he would never ask. Your job, on the kickoff team, is simple: run down the field as fast as you can, under control, running around and through blocks on the way, to finally bring down the ballcarrier. My adrenaline is spiking as I run out onto the field with L. J. Parker.

"This is a dream come true for you, Park," I tell him. "Lining up with the Paperboy." He laughs. The joke does more to break his tension than my own. I look to my right and see DeFalco, the Revs' slab of beef from before the game. He gives me the thumbs-up.

"Hit somebody, Kluck!" he shouts, from their sideline. These really are a classy bunch of guys. DeFalco, it should be noted, plays only on the Revs kickoff return team and plays without shoulder pads, opting only to wear a thin layer of foam underneath his jersey. He also wears running shoes.

My tenure as a defensive end is short-lived. The Revs score on a long pass play and I quickly line up to defend the two-point conversion.

"Don't let anything outside you, Kluck," says Haygood, who is lined up as the cornerback on my side. I am convinced that the Revs will run right at me, and dig in accordingly. The lineman across from me, Mike Pielech, is listed at 290 pounds. They would be crazy not to run at me. At the snap I bull rush Pielech, determined to lock out my arms and try to control him with my hands, keeping one eye on their scrambling quarterback. He throws at Haygood, who leaps in front of the ball and knocks it down. Just like that, my night is over.

Postgame, I realize that this is one of the few days in my life that has gone pretty much according to plan. After my series, the last seconds on the clock tick away and I scan the stands for my wife and son, my parents, and Chris and Beth. I motion for all of them to join me on the field for autographs. I feel as if, because I played, I have earned the right to sign a few of these tonight. The children, true to form, don't care about performance, they just want to be near a guy in a uniform. God bless them for making an old guy feel special. They have no idea what that means to us. I sign for a couple of kids, and then I sign for a guy in a wheelchair, who comments on how hard it must be for us to play on the turf. The irony of this statement almost brings me to tears—the fact that he probably has never run a day in his life but we dare to complain about running around on some bad turf, playing a child's game.

Both teams kneel down for the postgame prayer and I grab the hand next to me which belongs to Joe Bock who wears number 46 for the Revolution. Bock, I will learn, has suited up in five professional leagues and is a spry forty-six years of age. He is a large, distinguished-looking man with gray hair who probably goes about 6-foot-5 and 270 pounds. His hand engulfs mine.

"I'm the first guy to ever be traded in the GLIFL," he says, smiling. I don't think Bock even saw the field tonight which makes me sad. Ten hours is a long drive to stand on the sidelines, which I know all too well. "I started the season with the Rochester Raiders but didn't think I was getting enough playing time so I asked them to trade me to the Revolution."

Bock, who played collegiately at the University of Virginia, has suited up for the USFL's Birmingham Stallions and Houston Gamblers, the NFL's Buffalo Bills and St. Louis Cardinals, and finally the AFL's Chicago Bruisers in a pro career that lasted from 1981 to 1989. He played with Jim Kelly, Joe Cribbs, Cliff Stoudt, and Bruce Smith, and blocked against Lawrence Taylor when he was with the Bills.

"I never really got football out of my blood," he says. "I never officially retired from the NFL and I always had guys like Marv Levy commenting on what great shape I was in and how I could play for a long time. Now I teach and coach at an inner-city high school in Rochester and I scrimmage with the kids every day, without pads. So I joke to people that I've been playing high school ball for the last ten years."

I ask Bock how, after all of these years, he chose the GLIFL for his comeback.

"I saw the news reports about Mark Rypien coming to play a game for the Rochester Raiders at age forty-three and thought hey, if he can do it I know I can come back and play a game," he says. "But then as I started training I thought why just play in one game when I can play in all ten? My family was cool with it but then they know that I'm a little over the edge and crazy about football."

I ask Bock, finally, about his NFL experience. If living the dream that everyone here is chasing actually lived up to its billing.

"It wasn't really all I thought it would be," he says after some thought. "Almost every team I played for, from the Houston Gamblers in the USFL to the Bills, the players said that I was the best long snapper they ever saw. In 1987 I beat out about forty or fifty long snappers for the job with the Buffalo Bills. It was coming down to the last cut in camp and I thought I had the job won. But then the Chiefs cut a guy who played for [then Bills coach] Marv Levy in Kansas City, and he gave the job to that guy, who then got to snap in four Super Bowls. I couldn't help but think that it could have, and should have, been me snapping in those Super Bowls. I mean, I've been a Bills fan all my life. I was born and raised in Rochester."

My son, Tristan, has pilfered my helmet and is wearing it as he runs wind sprints up and down the field. He wipes out once, around the 20-yard line, and is picked up carefully by Revs QB Kevin Hanratty, who left the game in the third quarter after aggravating an ankle that he fractured three weeks ago. Hanratty still has a smile on his face and has quickly organized the kids into an impromptu game of touch. At this moment I think there will be a special place in heaven for Kevin Hanratty.

I am approached by Revs center Now-Allah James, who congratulates me on a good game. He looks exhausted. James is one of the smallest offensive linemen in the league but, like the rest of the Revs, fought hard and played a clean game.

"The travel is almost unbearable," he says. "I don't know if I can keep this up . . . the losing, I mean."

"But you're a pro football player," I tell him. "Not many people can say that."

I hope this makes him feel better. I'm realizing, tonight, that without an ability to make people feel better I don't really bring a whole lot to this equation.

I stop signing autographs long enough to drift back to my family, periodically, smiling from ear to ear, hoping this night will last forever but knowing it won't. I shoot a look at my wife and smile, hoping she'll share in this, the realization of my high school fantasies—great football game, beautiful girl in the stands (her), and all the rest. I half expect her to come sprinting across the threadbare

Astroturf and leap into my arms, right in front of the sign for Hungry Howie's Pizza. Cue Peter Gabriel song. Cue soft focus. I am the man. Instead, she looks downcast.

"What's wrong, baby?" I ask. Wondering why she isn't overcome with adulation because it is, in fact, *me* signing autographs.

"Playoffs," she replies. One word, and I understand.

After grabbing a pizza in the locker room for dad (thank you Hungry Howie's) I shower and slip back into the Charlestown Chiefs replica jersey from the movie *Slapshot* that I wore to the arena tonight. Many of the players have seen the movie and appreciate my homage to the minor league hockey classic.

"Nice jersey, Kluck," says Allsbury.

"We're living it," I tell him as I round the corner toward the parking lot and a long drive home.

The week after the NY/NJ win is one of my best in recent memory. I think back on the game often, and get the added gift of three CDs full of photos taken by my friend Jim Olson at the game. Olson is a physician and a budding sports photographer who has succeeded in making us all feel just a little bit special.

I get a phone call from L. J. Parker almost weekly now. We banter about practice, about end-zone celebrations, and about general team news. Parker's real reason for calling, however, is a desire to have access to the treasure trove of pictures taken by Olson. I instructed Jim to snap several pics of Parker and now he is ready to see them. I get the feeling that, for many of these guys, taking artifacts away from this experience, as proof that they existed here, is hugely important. Things like a Crunch T-shirt or a photograph can mean the world. I promise Parker that I'll burn him a CD, and make a mental note to contact Mike O'Brien, as well as make arrangements for several tickets for family and friends for the next game. I am gaining an appreciation for the minutia that real professional athletes deal with on a game-by-game basis. Arranging for tickets. Who is sitting where? Who is driving with whom? Will they know where to park? It's all a little exhausting on top of practice and writing.

I talk to Bob Kubiak briefly as well, to get an update on the status of the team and his relations with the league and Mike Powell. Kubiak, in a de facto sense, has taken over the running of the club, although Powell seems to have a desire to stay involved at some level.

"It looks like Mike has finally turned the ownership over to the league," Kubiak says. "But he's been spreading some rumors about me . . . I'd like to just sit down with the guy and get everything squared away. Basically the league has told him that if he walks away now, they won't come after any of the money he owes, which would be a pretty good deal for him. But there is some pride involved."

I can sense that Kubiak is stressed about this week's game. We need to beat Lehigh Valley again to insure our spot in the playoffs. But the teams are evenly matched and it will be a much tougher game than the one we just won. Made tougher because my devout wife is praying fervently for an Outlawz victory.

"We've lost Allsbury for the upcoming game," he says. "So I'm trying to find a defensive end and get a pass rush. I'm trying to get [Brian] Wright to commit."

Kubiak gives me the plan for practice and I let him go without suggesting to him that I might be able to provide a pass rush, based on my two series against NY/NJ. He's tired and I feel bad for taking any more of his time. He's already spending way too much time on the Battle Creek Crunch.

Later that night I meet a friend at a local pool where both of our kids are taking swimming lessons. He asks to see some pictures from the game and comments on the spatted shoes as we flip through.

"Why don't you do that to your shoes?" he asks, of the spats, the technique by which some of the players wrap tape around the outside of their shoes.

"You kind of have to be a good player, or at least a starter, to spat your shoes," I hear myself telling him. "When you're a backup or only play once in a while it would seem kind of silly to spat up, or wear a visor or whatever." What I'm describing is an informal pecking order that has always existed on football teams. I hadn't thought about it until now.

"You look good in these pictures," he says, I think, somewhat surprised. "You look legit. I mean, you look like a real player."

Parker calls again to make sure my agent is coming to the game. O'Brien currently represents a handful of guys at our level—guys who were good college players but for whatever reason haven't been able to take the next step. I have been with O'Brien when he was forced to fawn all over the parents of Memphis RB and blue chipper DeAngelo Williams, who summarily ignored him. Agenting, in this day and age, is a tough racket, but I really want to see my friend make it. The game would be just a little bit better if he did.

I have served as something of an advance scout for O'Brien, trying to sift through the chaff in our league to find some guys who might be able to take their games to the next level. I get asked at almost every practice—usually by Parker or Gills—when my agent is coming to a game. These guys have had other agent experiences before, usually with low-level operators who promise to send a couple of e-mails on their behalf and then forget about them. Part of being a decent athlete with a dream is reconciling yourself to being lied to, which starts with college recruiting and doesn't end until you're done playing sports.

I pick O'Brien up at his office on a Friday afternoon. He has agreed to meet with Parker and Gills, and is interested in signing them to the Standard Representation Contract. O'Brien works in downtown Lansing, in the legislative district where overly hair-gelled little political wonks roam the streets in new suits, looking falsely important chirping into cell phones. I would get eaten alive down here.

We meet them at a place called the Longhorn Steakhouse, where Parker, through his immeasurable charm, has somehow secured us a free lunch.

"You guys look like pro athletes or something," I tell Park and Gills as we wheel up. I get out and give them the perfunctory pro athlete handshake/hug, which I'm getting pretty good at if I do say so myself. O'Brien is nearly in tears because we've been laughing and quoting lines from Jerry McGuire to each other. O'Brien confides to me that he was worried for a long time that he didn't "look the part" of the sports agent. Rather, he is a married guy with kids, in his early forties, with a receding hairline and a friendly face. Better yet, he is sincere.

After we're seated, the wait staff immediately starts bringing out food. Chili-cheese fries, bread, pop, you name it. This is nice. Parker has convinced the staff here that we are somehow important. O'Brien has an easy way with the athletes and is honest with them, telling them tales about his near misses with first-round draft choices.

"I took four trips to Evansville, Indiana, to meet with Jay Cutler's dad, who was a lot like the Matt Cushman character in Jerry McGuire, right down to the Southern accent," he says. He goes on to describe how he routinely barbecued with Mr. Cutler, how they talked football and life, how O'Brien's Irish-Catholic father was a cop, as was Cutler's dad. He describes how Cutler's dad would fire question after question at him about draft and negotiation scenarios.

Finally, he describes the final visit, wherein Cutler's dad said, "Mike (pronounced *Mahk* in southern Indianian), you're one of our top-three selections. We're going to share the information with Jay and he'll make a choice."

Cutler, of course, went with a guy with an eighties mustache named Bus Cook who famously represents one Brett Favre.

"I was so depressed I went to the basement and played NCAA Football on the PlayStation for like forty-eight hours," Mike explains.

The guys laugh. They are impressed that he even got close to Jay Cutler. The group discusses workout strategies for Gills and Parker, about how we plan to connect them with a Big Ten–strength coach and perhaps give them access to Braylon Edwards's father, Stan, for world-class speed training. As big men who can run, Parker and Gills, we think, are extremely valuable commodities.

"We're just so glad to be playing football," says Parker. "I've had so many things get close and then fall through, like the Rampage and then the [Green Bay] Blizzard. I was starting to think I might never get on the field again. But when I suited up for the Crunch the first time I almost cried."

"Me too," adds Gills, the quieter of the two players.

"I really want to see you guys make it," I tell them. They have played too long, and taken too much of a beating for no money this season. I want to see them paid for their efforts and talents.

"This is the first client lunch I've ever had where the client picks up the tab!" O'Brien says to Parker, who charms everyone from the owner to the girls at the door on the way out. When you are in the presence of L. J. Parker you feel like you're in the presence of a professional athlete, and people like that.

Parker shakes his hand and looks him directly in the eye.

"I was trying to make an impression," he says.

Game 8: Battle Creek Crunch versus Lehigh Valley Outlawz

Somewhere along I-94, driving to the game, it hits me that this is almost over. After tonight we are on the road in Port Huron, and then back home for one last game against the New York/New Jersey Revolution, which will probably be my last shot at significant playing time. This is one of the last times I will make the left onto Hamblin Avenue, wheel my car into the parking garage, and carry my bag around the back to the unmarked players' entrance.

As I pull up tonight I see the Lehigh Valley Outlawz getting off their modified RV. After they disembark I hop up on the bumper to get a look inside. It is your garden-variety RV (like Mom and Pop might buy after retiring and drive around to any number of grim Midwestern campsites) that has been gutted of its faux-wood paneling and chintzy sink, to be replaced by twenty-four standard bus seats. The

Outlawz (I still hate that "z") must have been wedged in here like sardines. It looks miserable.

Jim DePaul, their owner, catches me looking inside and we get a chance to visit.

"Great bus, Jim," I tell him, bending the truth just a little. It would be a great bus for a two-hour trip, as opposed to an eleven-hour trip. "You guys did a nice job with this."

Like the other league owners I've had a chance to meet, he is still friendly and enthusiastic about the venture. DePaul, from a financial standpoint, has been one of the most successful owners in the league, drawing between three to four thousand fans to Stabler Arena for home games. We talk about the Crunch's recent dramas.

"Don't write anything bad about all of this," he implores me. This is a refrain that has reared its head of late. When I checked into the Crunch office this afternoon about tickets, Bob Kubiak said, "Give this guy whatever he wants." I told Kubiak he was too good to me, to which he replied: "I don't want you to trash us in the book."

"This turf is horrible," says DePaul, as we walk the perimeter of the arena, and look over at the sections of Astroturf duct-taped together in the end zone.

"It's hard as a rock," says wide receiver Billy "Superman" Parker, who has sidled up next to us, and bends down to rap his knuckles on the green carpet. Parker was the player who ran onto the field in a Superman cape when we played these guys a couple of weeks ago. Like all good receivers, even his pregame warm-up attire looks meticulously chosen. He rolls out of the locker room in a form-fitting Superman T-shirt, with Under Armour armbands wrapped around his "guns" at varying levels. There is also a bandanna. Superman very much looks the part of a pro receiver. He is tall and lanky, and looks not unlike Snoop Dogg. I am also disappointed to find that he is an exceedingly nice guy.

"I played a little community college ball," he says, telling me a story that could have come straight out of the Battle Creek Crunch locker room. "But then I ended up playing a couple of seasons of semipro and was an All-Star both years. Jim offered me the opportunity to come out here and play and make a little money." He pauses for a moment to collect his thoughts. "But I would play for nothing," he continues. "I do it for this," he says, sweeping a huge officially licensed gloved hand over the expanse of Kellogg Arena's empty seats. "Coming out here and playing in front of the fans every week, this is what you dream about as a kid. That's what it's all about."

I don't have the heart to tell him that most of the seats will probably still be empty at game time.

"I shared some marketing ideas with Bob," says DePaul, who seems to intuitively read my thoughts re: the empty seats. "The key is community involvement. Every time there's another event here at Kellogg, there should be Crunch banners up, and you should have players and dancers at the door signing autographs and handing out tickets."

I tell DePaul that I have yet to see a poster, or a T-shirt for that matter. We agree that Powell, while a nice guy with good intentions, overestimated the drawing power of a team here—thinking that if he simply opened the doors there would be a sellout every week.

About 50 feet away from us, Bob Kubiak is disgustedly flipping through a Crunch game program (sale price, five dollars). The program features about thirty-five pages of ads, plus one page on the Illegal Motion dancers and three pages of Crunch player photos.

"Gone. Gone. Gone," says Kubiak, flipping through the photos, which were taken in the preseason. There are seven players left from that original group—Dolph, me, Ches, Parker, Pettaway, Lacksheide, and Gardner. Everybody else is gone and for some reasons the Brothers Kubiak, our two quarterbacks, were never photographed.

"We can't sell these," Kubiak tells our GM, who for the second-straight week is nattily attired in a black suit. He looks like he's going to a wedding. "Just give them away at the door, but rip the player photo section out first. The kids can just use the back pages to get autographs."

In the locker room I discover that L. J. Parker has a Superman plan of his own. He has purchased some black fabric and painted on a Superman logo with his number, 5, in the middle. He plans to wear the getup out onto the field during the pregame player introductions. He and Richard Gills are eating pizza and throwing bottled water at each other. Gills goes berserk when Parker splashes some water on the crotch of his khaki shorts.

"Man, these are my school shorts!" he says, furious.

"Can I see the cape, Park?" I ask.

"No, I'm keeping it in the bag until the introductions," he says, conspiratorially. "Maybe you can help me put it on right before then."

I nod in the affirmative, and then continue getting dressed—the jock first, then the black tights, the silky black game pants, thigh pads, undershirt, ankle wraps, black shoes, and bandanna. I'm invoking Ches tonight, with a black do-rag under the helmet.

"Kluck looks ready to go!" says Azriel Woodson, who is eating from a box of Popeye's fried chicken that he brought to the locker room. Woodson used to wear a suit to each home game, but today he wears a LaCrosse Night Train warm-up suit, which he snagged from one of the many professional indoor teams he has been a part of. I'm pretty sure he's mocking me.

Out on the field I toss balls with quarterback Kenny Kubiak, and we both comment on the fact that we're only an hour and a half away from game time and most of our team hasn't shown up yet.

"I got here at 4:15 and felt late," he says. "I always feel like if I run late I'm going to get here and everybody is going to be dressed and doing a walk-through or something."

It's a recurring nightmare I have occasionally. That I am supposed to play a football game but arrive late, only to deal with myriad equipment problems and miss the game entirely.

"What are you doing next year? You going to try to play somewhere again?" he asks.

I tell him no, that my wife would probably come after me with a nine millimeter if I even hinted at playing again. But it makes me feel good to know that he thinks I *could* play someplace next year. I tell him that if the Crunch, or another team, needed a body in practice that I would be happy to do that. The idea of this being over in a couple of weeks has already started to sink in and that feeling sucks. In a few weeks I'll go back to being just another guy.

"I missed my son Grant's big baseball tournament last week," he says. "I was driving to practice Wednesday with Eric Gardner and I got a call from Tim who just told me not to go. He said nobody would show up and I'd just end up getting pissed off anyway. So I turned around but with traffic and everything I ended up missing the whole game. Grant had a triple and drove in a bunch of runs and I missed it.

"My body doesn't feel right either," he continues. "When I have to chase after a ball on a bad snap and end up getting hit it starts hurting immediately and hurts for a week. Some weeks I'm nervous and I'm really into it, but today I don't feel much of anything."

As the minutes tick down toward game time, the rest of the players begin filing in. Smitty and B-Wright (the two non-twin defensive ends who look exactly alike) have made the trip from Detroit, along with Shaun Blackmon. They arrive forty minutes or so before game time. Even Ches, who is usually dressed in full uniform three hours before warm-ups, is running late today. I think not getting paid is wearing thin.

After pulling my black game jersey over my shoulder pads, I settle into my regular spot in the locker room between Kyle Lacksheide and Tyler Paesens. We don't have actual lockers—just pegs on the wall and a folding chair—so we have just taken to occupying the same spaces week after week. Football players are creatures of habit. I often wonder why I chose this seat—in between two of the fattest, and meanest, players on the team. Lacksheide is eyeing the tags on my equipment bag, and a piece of red ribbon tied around the handle. I can tell he wants to say something insulting because Kyle Lacksheide is pretty easy to read. Subtlety isn't his forte, so much.

"What's with the Merry Christmas ribbon on your bag, Kluck?" he says derisively. Paesens perks up beside me, ready to jump on the insult train as well. "It's left over from when we traveled to Europe," I tell him, bracing for what's next.

"Europe? What were you doing there?" he asks.

"We lived there, for a year," I reply. "In Lithuania . . . it's part of the former Soviet Union," I add, patronizingly, feeling immediately like a pompous ass.

Lacksheide comments that it's just like that movie *The Hostel*, which we watched on one of our never-ending bus rides earlier this season. Pretty scary stuff, says Lacksheide. It is without a doubt the worst movie I have ever seen, in which American students are stranded and killed in a dank, Eastern European hostel.

"I bet the women there are beautiful," says Lacksheide.

"They sometimes stare at themselves in the mirror when they smoke," I tell him, trying to sound profound.

Finally Paesens joins in.

"You think you're better than us Teddy, because you've lived in Europe?" he asks, rhetorically. "F—k you."

Some random game-day observations from the sideline:

I have the pleasure of seeing Kyle Lacksheide's brother sitting in the first row, above the Crunch bench, and he looks just like a freshman-in-high-school version of Kyle Lacksheide. Buzz cut. Aviator sunglasses. Preppy-but-too-tight polo shirt and "you-want-a-piece-of-this" look in his eye. He is there with a couple of prettiest-girl-in-school types (fake tans, lots of makeup) and a buddy. I spend a couple of minutes studying him and predicting out the next few years of his life in my mind—the All-Conference selection, the inevitable Pontiac Grand Am, and the dalliances with alcohol that will come via his older brother.

I am also finding myself driven crazy by the music tonight. There's something profoundly annoying about techno music throbbing around in an empty room. It seems to bounce directly off the empty seats and go right into the frontal lobe of my brain, like an ice-cream headache. I will have snippets of the songs "Ridin' Dirty,"

"Whatcha Gonna Do with All That Junk Inside That Trunk?," and "Welcome to the Jungle" burned into my brain forever as a result of this season. It's like playing football in an empty nightclub. I ask a few other teammates if it's bothering them, and they agree. We're all getting old, I think.

"I'm not feeling this tonight," says Smitty. "I think not getting paid has a lot to do with it. When I decided to do this at thirty-six years old it was the chance to play professionally and get paid . . . I mean I love playing but I've played semipro for free, for a lot of years."

I agree, and tell Smitty, a successful warehouse manager, that this is starting to feel a lot like semipro.

"Exactly!" he says. "When I started Powell promised me 250 bucks a game, which covers a lot of the gas coming from Monroe and leaves me a little something left over. Now I'm out here putting my body on the line for nothing. The fire is gone. When I started doing this, like when we went up to Marion and won, the fire was back. But I haven't been excited like that in a few weeks. That's why I didn't come last week. You can put that in the book. I'd like to find Mike Powell and kick his ass."

The thought of Smitty getting ahold of Mike Powell is not a pretty one. Just then Ashe comes by and smacks Smitty on the rump. "I need you tonight!" he shouts, shaking his fist. I feel bad for both men. Ashe is just working to keep the ship afloat and Smitty is trying to find it in his heart to play a violent game that no longer appeals to him. I hope he doesn't get hurt tonight.

One of their chubby linemen shanks the opening kickoff and we are rewarded with stellar field position.

"He's lining up soccer style but he's going to kick with his toe!" cracks our kicker, Brad Selent, upon seeing the sad kickoff.

The Outlawz look to have literally beefed up their starting line since we last played; they have added a couple of fatties named Lloyd Brooks (330 pounds) and Alan Stokes (290 pounds) to their rotation. Unfortunately, their prodigious trash talking matches the girth underneath their jerseys—these cats have been woofing to our bench ever since player introductions. I fear that it's going to be a long, and chippy, night.

After getting the ball on the 10-yard line but still failing to score on our first drive, the Lehigh Valley Outlaws (I refuse, from this point, to type the "z" because it feels ridiculous. Frank DeFord wouldn't type the "z") cram the ball down our throats courtesy of what seems like about twenty-five running plays by flanker Steve Cook—a diminutive white guy with the number 4 on his jersey.

Their newfound running attack is a result of an injury to their starting QB Chad Schwenk, who leads the league in several passing categories. Schwenk pulled his groin kicking in warm-ups. Selent and I saw him—who bears a striking resemblance to our former receiver Donnie Lonsway—hobble into the locker room after kicking a few long field goals, his evening prematurely ended.

Unfortunately, we now have to deal with the presence of Cook, and their new quarterback, a glorified running back named Keeno Theadford, whose two responsibilities seem to be handing off to Cook, and making our defense look silly on designed quarterback keepers.

We are also without the services of coach-turned-defensive end Anthony Allsbury tonight. Allsbury, in addition to handling personnel changes on the lines and calling line stunts, has also infused our defense with a pass rush that would have come in handy against the elusive Theadford.

"He's across the street at a bachelor party," says L. J. Parker. I can only manage to raise an eyebrow. Everybody deals with not getting paid in different ways, I hear myself telling Parker, unsure of why I am defending Allsbury. Parker has the added motivation of spotting my agent in the stands tonight. He has come to watch Parker, Gills, and Gardner in hopes of signing up some new talent. Parker promises fireworks.

Our defense gets pounded by the run, but we are kept in the game courtesy of long scoring strikes from Tim Kubiak to Richard Gills. This is something of a coming out party for Gills. He scores on strikes of 25 and 19 yards in the first quarter, and another 30 yarder in the second, to keep the game within reach. Gills, at least tonight, is owning his man and owning the corner of the end zone, where he routinely goes up to snatch footballs out of the air.

"We're going to run out of balls tonight," I remark to Kenny Kubiak on the sideline. He knows exactly what I'm talking about.

"Gills," is all he says in response. Gills is famous for pilfering footballs after touchdowns, two-point conversions, or catching a routine 6-yard out. He seems to be operating under the misconception that this team is actually making money.

I am also surprised talking to a stat guy, who reveals that Tim Kubiak is actually leading the league in passing yards and is second only to Rochester's Matt Cottengim in TD passes. He has come a long way since those first two games, when Ashe thought he was shaving points.

At halftime we trudge into the locker room, looking like a team that's a step slow, and playing like a team that hasn't been paid. Ashe comes in swearing and throws a marker at the dry-erase board.

"Chase, go take a walk or something," Tyler Paesens says to our water boy, who is seven years old. "It's gonna get a little nasty in here."

Chase stands in place for a moment, enraptured by what he's seeing. He doesn't want to leave the inner sanctum, even if that sanctum is going to teach him phrases he shouldn't be familiar with until at least high school. I send him on an imaginary errand to find his dad.

"We're getting our asses tapped!" shouts Ashe, before turning to diagram something on the greaseboard. He has devised a way to stop the Lehigh Valley running game.

"We're cool," says Coach Kubiak, calmly, playing the good cop to Ashe's bad cop. "Just keep playing. Just keep doing what we're doing and we'll be fine."

"You keep your head!" says Ashe to Lacksheide, who has already received a personal foul and a message from the officiating staff that he will be thrown out and suspended if he gets another one. Lack is one of those players who on winning teams is called "nasty" and "a warrior" and on losing teams is unfortunately just a little dirty.

"I gotta get one in every game coach, just to let 'em know I'm playing," says Lacksheide. Ashe is not amused this time. He knows that if we lose Lack our offense will be screwed in a serious way.

"Hey, Coach," says Paesens to Ashe. "When are you gonna suit up?" It seems an odd question for an odd time. Ashe thinks about it for a moment.

"Never," he answers, shifting into Zen mode. "I know my limitations, brother."

The second half seems to bring nothing but more darkness to the dim confines of Kellogg Arena. First, L. J. Parker is ejected on a questionable call along the wall. Parker, who was pursuing backside on a toss play, drove his forearm into the head of Keeno Theadford, who lost his helmet and flew over the boards, much to the delight of the Crunch faithful. Unfortunately, this officiating crew had been calling the game tight with quick whistles along the boards. After a short conference they thought it best to eject Parker, who threw his helmet down in disgust, the plastic making a sharp crack as it caromed off the hard green turf. He makes his way to the bench and immediately peels off his shoulder pads and jersey, a sinister look on his face as he paces the perimeter of the field.

An Eric Gardner plunge from the 1-yard line, followed by a Tim Kubiak sneak in a subsequent series puts us up 36–28 early in the fourth quarter, but the excitement is short-lived because Keeno Theadford soon takes control. He runs and passes his team to three scores in the fourth quarter, which seals it for the Outlawz, despite a Tim Kubiak to Eric Gardner bomb with nine ticks left on the clock.

Theadford was sensational, finishing with 91 yards and a score through the air, added to another 48 yards and three touchdowns on the ground.

The other scary moment came as we were trying (in vain) to score again with just a few seconds remaining. Tim Kubiak aired a long ball out for WR Brian Dolph, who, racing after the ball near the back of the end zone, flipped violently over the end wall. The arena immediately hushed, including the pounding techno music, as team Dr. Tom Martinez raced around to attend to him. I followed Martinez around the boards, and found Dolph lying prostrate on the concrete floor.

His wife and young son always sit in the same place on the front row, and she, to me, seems a perfect football wife. Appropriately excited for him, but usually not too concerned about the day-to-day pounding he absorbs as a pro receiver.

We are encouraged to see Dolph moving his legs after a few moments, and he is eventually helped into the locker room by Smitty, B-Wright, and Martinez, who informs me that his leg is just badly bruised. I immediately deliver that word to his wife, over the rail, and she looks immeasurably relieved. As for me, it's just nice to feel helpful tonight.

Number of practices this week, between our game against Lehigh Valley and our game versus the 8–0 Port Huron Pirates: 0

I get a chance to chat with Richard Gills about this during the week.

"I talked to Kubiak and we're on our own for transportation up to Port Huron," he says. It seems our team, literally, is limping to the finish line.

Chapter Ten

A Prayer for Chesaurae Rhodes

Game 9: Battle Creek versus Port Huron

"Hey Dicklips, where are you?" says Kyle Lacksheide into his two-way cell phone. It is 4:30 on the day of the Port Huron game and Lacksheide, Parker, and I are the only players who have arrived for the 7:00 game. Doc Martinez and Sean, The Intern/GM nervously pace the spacious locker room. It's a hockey locker room so the floor is covered with those rubber mats, and there is a greaseboard with hockey strategies attached to the wall.

"I'm lost," says Tim Kubiak, through Lacksheide's phone. "I'm trying to find this place."

"Good story," says Lacksheide, obviously unmoved.

"I like that good story thing," says Parker, "I'm gonna start using that."

Out on the field it appears that Port Huron has about fifty-five players dressed for the game. They are all out on the turf in matching T-shirts and shorts, throwing the ball, goofing off, and clowning like good, confident teams clown. I meet a couple of their practice squad players, Brian Towns and John Spadafore, along the boards. They are both huge linemen who, apparently, haven't dressed for a game all season.

"They take pretty good care of you guys here?" I ask them, expecting them to gush about the team-provided housing and all the other perks.

"Not really," says Spadafore. "Most of the money goes to the stars. Rayshawn gets the league maximum, three hundred dollar per game, plus a three-hundred win bonus. I also heard he gets a cut of all of the T-shirt sales and his contract has a provision that he gets a certain number of carries per game and a certain number of carries inside the 5-yard line."

I look across the faded green carpet to starting running back Rayshawn Askew, who is goofing around with teammates. He's wearing a white "wife beater" and looks ridiculously huge. It's going to be a long night.

"Well, as far as I'm concerned, we've got extra uniforms in the locker room and you guys can play for us tonight," I tell Spadafore and Towns, filling them in on some of our roster and paycheck troubles.

"It's that bad?" Towns asks.

"Yeah, probably worse," I respond. Kicker Brad Selent has arrived, along with lineman Harry Pettaway, who brought a box of athletic tape and some Gatorade to contribute to the cause.

"Who were those guys?" asks Selent.

"A couple of guys from Port Huron's practice squad," I reply.

"They have a practice squad?"

"Yeah, it's pretty cool, their team has practices and everything," I reply, sarcastically, using humor to mask the fact that I think Port Huron might score 100 points on us tonight.

Back inside the locker room, players are beginning to arrive, but we're still well below the nineteen we need to field a complete team.

"We only need seven," says Lacksheide, emphatically. "I'll play both ways. If I had played both ways all year we sure as hell wouldn't be 3–5."

"Yeah, we'd be 1–7," says Martinez, after the requisite comedic pause. Doc is still wearing his swim trunks from the beach, where I ran into him earlier today.

"I knew that was coming," says Lack, who just enjoys banter for the sake of banter. This conversation was just a prelude to a long series of questions to the Doc about such subjects as why your cock shrinks when you swim in cold water, and how many vaginal exams he got to perform as a medical student. Lacksheide and Tyler Paesens are enraptured. This, clearly, is good stuff.

Donnie Lonsway, who was released after the first game of the season, comes through the door looking like, well, Donnie Lonsway (bearded, scraggly, unkempt). I am sincerely glad to see him; he was one of my favorite teammates from camp.

"What time did you get the call. Donnie?" asks Kenny Kubiak.

"About one-thirty this afternoon," he replies. "So I just said, 'What the hell?'."

Kubiak just shakes his head. His attitude through all this has been relentlessly positive, but I think it's starting to wear him down. Like the rest of us, he's afraid of what might happen tonight.

"I don't know about you," he says, "but I'm not sure I even want to get in tonight. I mean, not practicing and everything, I don't know how good I'd be, plus my body just hurts for a week from taking one hit."

The subject of quarterbacking has been a topic of much discussion amongst the players, who are unfairly blaming Tim Kubiak's fumble for the loss last week. But when Kubiak has protection and a full arsenal (Gardner, Gills, Dolph) of good receivers at his disposal he has been nearly unstoppable. The critiques don't seem to phase him though, as he saunters into the locker room and slumps down in front of a stall. Timmy is a preppie, in khaki shorts and a golf shirt, your classic 1980s star-of-the-school type of quarterback. He looks ready to go to a barbecue in the suburbs.

"I've got mixed feelings about the playing, too," I tell Ken Kubiak. Since I tasted real action against New York/New Jersey, I am craving more, but playing tonight against Port Huron's line stocked with NCAA Division I stars could get me killed. Even so, I am relatively relaxed before game time. I will do whatever I can to get on the field, and tonight that might mean playing special teams.

Truthfully, I have added motivation this week. Shortly after this book deal was announced, a newspaper reporter in Port Huron decided that he would join their team as a practice squadder and blog about the experience for his paper's Web site. He also wanted to collect material for a book of his own. Yes, it is a free country and I encourage this guy to fulfill his writing dreams, but I would also like to knock his block off tonight. If I can't be the toughest player in the league I can at least prove that I am the toughest writer by knocking the crap out of this joker. I shared this sentiment with my wife and she thought I was silly. "Don't do anything stupid and get yourself hurt," she said, adding: "But if you get a clean shot at him definitely light him up." What a woman.

Out on the field, Bob Kubiak looks as outwardly stressed as I've seen him, pacing the carpet and taking calls on his cell phone, trying to connect with potential players and league officials. I ask him about his week.

"Believe it or not, Mike Powell is still trying to exert some control over this team," he says. "He's trying to say that he has some claim to any sponsorship dollars that come in at this point. I'm like 'Mike this isn't your team anymore.'" We both agree that for Powell to walk away without a lawsuit at this point would have to be, for him, a moral victory.

"We've got some guys on this team who are . . . for lack of a better term . . . trying to do the thug thing now," he says. "They're figuring 'hey we're not practicing and we're not getting paid so Kubiak needs me now.' They feel like they have leverage so they can go around with their jerseys untucked and all of that [Aside: Every coach I've ever played for has been unhealthily obsessed with players tucking in their jerseys. Why?]. And to a certain extent, they're right. But there are guys who have been around and seen all of this semipro stuff before, like Pettaway, Timmy, Lonsway, and some of the other guys. Lack and TP are pros, and so is Herb Haygood. We needed Eric Gardner tonight but supposedly he has a back problem or something . . . I never called B-Wright or Smitty because I know they're pissed off about the money thing.

"But look around here," he says, "this [McMorran Place] is a professional arena. They've got a staff of eight people running this operation. I have Sean."

We are approached by a league official asking for finalization of our roster . . . while half of our team is yet to show up. Kubiak looks at me for a beat, and then turns to the official and begins rattling off names and numbers. The official, after some scribbling, walks away placated.

"I just made half of those names up," he says, with a half grin. We chat a little while longer before Kubiak leaves me with this: "Be ready tonight, we might need you." My sphincter constricts.

I run into Scott Ashe on the way back into the locker room. Ashe has been quietly critical of the operation since the beginning but always positive on game days.

"We've gotta dance with what we've got," he says, shaking his head, "but this is embarrassing. Mike Powell really screwed this team over. When Bob called me to coach I said, 'Bob, I don't know, this guy is a slapdick', but he assured me that everything would be okay."

Back in the locker room, Doc is still holding court with Lack and Paesens. He pulls on a rubber glove before applying Biofreeze to the leg of kicker Brad Selent, who has taken a beating making special-teams tackles in recent weeks. Paesens, seeing the rubber glove, senses an opportunity.

"Doc, you wouldn't even get halfway to my prostate with those little hands," he says. I laugh out loud.

It's hot on the field, really hot, and the music feels like it's going to pound a hole in my skull. As the defensive linemen are in the corner of the end zone warming up, somebody points at Ches, who is lying on the turf and twitching, just like seizure victims on television. I have never seen this in person. There is shouting. We all run to Ches's side and motion for the Doc. We shout to the press box to cut the music as Doc holds Ches's head in his hands. I immediately begin to pray. "Lord, be with my friend, give peace to his family, and guide the doctor's hands."

Ches's wife rushes down from the stands with their two small children, who don't understand what's going on. Along with big Tyler Paesens and Pettaway, I distract the kids, asking them questions and playing catch off to the side. "Daddy's just taking a rest," we tell them. "He's tired." There is more pacing and more praying as the players huddle in groups while the paramedics rush in and strap

Ches to a gurney. One of Ches's kids catches me kneeling with my eyes closed, while I pray for his dad.

"Are you sleeping?" he asks, his big dark eyes staring up at me. I want to cry and go home to be with my son. The last place I want to be is here, in this fiery furnace packed with hostile fans. "Yeah buddy, I was just taking a little rest, just like dad," I tell him.

Ches is wheeled away and I rap him on the thigh pad and give him a thumbs-up. He is paralyzed on the left side; his left arm, leg, and face are slack. I go over to the wall where my wife is sitting with a couple of friends, Detta and Zandy. I give them the thumbs-up and ask them to pray for Ches. Really, I just wanted to be close to my family for a second.

In thirty minutes, we will be playing football.

In the locker room there is a frantic search to find helmets for two big defensive linemen who have just arrived from Detroit. They are of the same build, about 6-foot-5 and 270 pounds. I have never seen either of them before, ditto for a big white nose tackle named Wiersma who we brought in today as well. Wiersma looks like an older guy, and he's practically frothing at the mouth with excitement. He's pounding his head on lockers and talking about what he's going to do. It strikes me as cartoonish, and the rest of us, who have been around all season, just roll our eyes at him.

The locker room is as sullen as I've ever seen it before a game. Kubiak, I think, doesn't know what to say and I don't blame him.

"Some of you guys that think you can play," he says, "who think you haven't gotten opportunities. This is your chance to prove yourselves. We're going to go out there and try to control the ball. Try to keep their offense off the field."

Ches's seizure has created a domino effect of problems. Foremost, we have no kick returner now, and we are down one receiver— Herb Haygood is essentially playing on one leg (with a high ankle sprain on the other) and is focusing on defense.

As we file somberly out of the locker room, I pass a depressed-looking Doc in the tunnel.

"I felt so helpless out there, Teddy," he says, as I put my arm around him.

"You did the best you could, Doc," I say. "You took care of him. Just pray for him now, and I will, too. That's all we can do."

I then run out of the tunnel, like I've dreamed of doing as a child and an adult, to a chorus of boos.

The Port Huron player introductions seem to take forever. As a song by Drowning Pool throbs through the building, each player is introduced by name, jersey number, position, and college. They all strut and peacock out of the tunnel in much the same manner as I have seen all year. I'm struck by how tired I'm getting of player introductions. Some jump up and down, some dance, some crawl through the tunnel of cheerleaders. It's all been done before. There is nothing new under the sun.

"The introductions at the football games are my least-favorite part," my wife said to me, today at the beach. "They turn out all the lights, except for some crazy strobe light, crank up the testosterone-pumping music to give the greatest impact, I guess, to the player's antics. As each player's name is called, they come racing, dancing, strutting, or prancing out to the field, the more ridiculous their intro dance, the more impressed we are all supposed to be, I guess. Rather than being impressed by this show of confidence, I am repulsed by the chest-pounding, self-focused, spotlight-grabbing, cry-for-attention immaturity—these are supposed to be grown men? The whole performance brings to mind little children, shouting empty boasts at each other on the playground."

"Ouch," I replied. "I'm glad you don't think less of me for it . . . you don't, right?"

I am especially intrigued by another high priced indoor legend, quarterback Shane Franzer. Franzer played for the Ohio Valley Greyhounds of the National Indoor Football League during the 2002 through 2004 seasons. He was the MVP of the 2003 NIFL Championship game, when the Greyhounds won their second-consecutive Indoor Bowl over the Utah Warriors, 45–37.

Franzer attended Ohio Northern University, where he compiled numerous school records in three years with the Polar Bears. His stats for all-time total offense (6,731 yards), touchdown passes (58), and quarterback-rushing yards (1,089) rank as the best in ONU history. He also holds the single-season records for total yards (2,862), touchdown passes (27), and quarterback rushing yards (500).

He is a stud, and looks the part of the slightly hardened career minor-leaguer, traveling from town to town in search of a paycheck and small-town adulation. He has a gigantic, Harbaugh-esque jawline, and looks not unlike one of those old nutcracker toys your grandparents have sitting on the mantle during the holiday season. I imagine him sitting in a small, white-walled apartment somewhere in Port Huron, dreaming about the NFL or not dreaming about the NFL. The thought makes me sad either way. The fact that his team is about to destroy us makes me even more sad.

"This is the best team money can buy," says Azriel Woodson as they shimmy out of the tunnel. There still seems to be about fifty of them. I take a spot on the bench beside Kenny Kubiak, who wears a look of both disgust and fear on his face. It's going to be a really long evening.

The closest I come to getting injured in the first half is straining my neck to keep one eye on the game clock on a scoreboard that hangs from the arena ceiling. Our first drive is encouraging in that we score and in the process milk nearly seven minutes off the clock. We use a mixture of running plays and short slants to Rich Gills and Donnie Lonsway, who catches the first TD pass.

The next forty-five minutes is a blur of Port Huron touchdowns that I won't describe in much detail here. Suffice it to say that it is 49–7 Port Huron at halftime, and nobody is having much fun at all. Wiersma, along with the other two defensive linemen, is getting pushed around like he's on skates. I guess he should have pounded his head against the lockers a few more times, ratcheting up the intensity.

I have taken a different approach to the hecklers behind our bench tonight. Glancing over my right shoulder I get a glimpse of two quintessential frat-boy types wearing button-down oxfords and trophy blondes on their respective arms. They are also downing cheap domestic beers as if their lives depended on it. This, I think, might make an already sucky night even suckier. I decide to just be proactive and I walk over to them and begin chatting.

The frat kid ends up being charming. He asks me questions about the team, and I end up basically spilling my guts about the type of season we've had. He is shocked to hear about our ownership foibles, and the fact that I couldn't tell him the names of half of my teammates tonight. We end up chatting periodically throughout the night, and I can't help but think his affinity for the underdog grew, while his opinion of his own bought-and-paid-for heroes might have diminished somewhat.

On our way into the locker room at halftime I grab Sean Lalonde, who gives me a halfhearted high five.

"Sean, go talk to Jeff from the league and see if you can get them to keep the clock running in the second half. This is embarrassing."

Sean agrees, and as he leaves, Ches's wife and kids enter the locker room to give an update and retrieve his stuff.

"Ches is okay," she says. "He's moving around and all of his blood work and tests came back clear. He asked for his bandanna, jersey, and gloves."

I go to look for Ches's gear and finally find it on top of one of the lockers. I grab the jersey and gloves but am stopped by a firm hand on my arm.

"Don't give him the jersey," says Doc Martinez. There is more, I think, to the Chesaurae Rhodes story than I am fully aware.

The second half is a blur as Pirates running back and University of Cincinnati product Rayshawn Askew scores about eighty-six rushing touchdowns. The Pirates keep their starters in for the entirety of the second half and seem more than happy to run up the score. I just hope they don't reach 100.

Their PA announcer (recently added to a short list of people I would like to kill) announces that he has set a new league record for rushing TD's, rushing yards, rushing attempts, and consecutive touchdown dances. Hooray. Run clock, run. They also have a guy dressed as a Pirate waving a plastic sword in the air as he runs around the perimeter of the arena. I later learn that his name is Brian and that for years he has been studying "pirate culture" and begged the Pirates brass for this chance to dress up as the stereotypical pirate (eye patch, sword, wooden leg) and cavort around the arena. There is probably a humorless political action group in Vermont that lobbies against stereotyping of pirates (next, on NPR!), and I think they need to know about Brian.

We struggle mightily in the second half because our better players—Parker, Gills, Pettaway, and Lacksheide—have been pressed into both-ways duty and are exhausted while Port Huron is constantly rotating fresh legs in front of them.

Tim Kubiak is struggling again as well. He is spraying balls all over the arena—overthrowing receivers and throwing balls into the carpet. He is rushed, and receives a pounding from the Port Huron defensive line that includes another indoor legend named Eddie Bynes who once had twenty-nine sacks in an indoor season playing in another small town for another small team.

The only thing I care to remember about the second half is that I get to play on the kickoff and kickoff return teams. These special teams, where the running is fast and the field is wide open, are among the most dangerous jobs on a football field. But they are also the most fun.

I can see Kubiak searching for me on the bench, and I pull on my dry helmet, the pads of which uncomfortably tug against the dry hair on my head. But I'm jacked about the chance to go in and this, responding to Kubiak's looks immediately, with no hesitation, might be what I'm most proud of about this experience. I have regained the ability to be decisive and, at times, bold. Normally, in high school and college, I'd be racked with nervousness. I spent those years as a knee-bouncing ball of overwrought nervous energy, which made every practice monumental in both scope and misery. I loved football but despised and fought against my own raw nerves. I would be in the bathroom every fifteen minutes before games or even practice, feeling the nervous energy drain out of me—leaving me feeling flat when it was time to perform. Now there is nothing.

I race down the field on two separate occasions, and am thrilled to feel the turf under my feet as I lock up with Port Huron linebacker Ruben Gay on a kickoff, and defensive back Jeremiah McLaurin on a kick return. In the grand scheme of the game they are two wholly insignificant plays, but they have made my night a thrilling one because I have again played professional football.

Jogging off the field I catch a thumbs-up from my hecklers-turned-friends and send a wave up to my wife, son, and friends in section 18. I can see Tristan driving a toy car up and down the arena steps and I want desperately to be with him now. Final score 69–7.

Considering the fact that Ches is once again healthy, and we got out of Port Huron without losing anyone else to injury, the night could have been much, much worse.

"Hey, if you guys beat New Jersey next week and Marion loses, you'll be back here for the playoffs!" The voice belongs to an excited Jeff Spitaleri, who is trying to make me feel better. I have a slice of pizza in my hand, my bag slung over my shoulder, and have just beat a hasty retreat out of the locker room in hopes of racing to my car and holing up in the hotel room with my wife and son as soon as possible. I give him a halfhearted thumbs-up and mumble something about calling him this week. The idea of driving back here for another shellacking isn't exactly a happy one. I hope I wasn't rude.

Acting partly as L. J. Parker's friend, and partly as an agent, I send the following e-mail to former Indiana University head coach and current San Diego Chargers offensive coordinator, Cam Cameron:

From: Ted Kluck
To: Cameron, Cam
Sent: Tue Jun 20 13:17:41 2006
Subject: LJ Parker

Dear Coach Cameron,

I had the privilege of playing a season of professional indoor football this summer with one of your former Indiana University players, WR/LB LJ Parker.

While Parker is a friend and a teammate first, he has also been the subject of much of my writing, in a series of columns that appeared on ESPN.com Page 2 and will eventually become my second nationally-published book. (see link)

http://sports.espn.go.com/espn/page2/story?page = kluck/060411

Parker is a 6' 2" 230 LB (4.55 40yd) who is currently third in the Great Lakes Indoor Football League in tackles, fourth in tackles for loss, and in the top ten in sacks. More importantly, he has been a defensive captain in every game, has contributed on offense as a WR, played hurt, and has generally exhibited a great attitude the entire season.

That said, I wondered if this may be the time of year to get LJ, still only 25, a workout with the San Diego Chargers? I would think a guy with his size, speed and ability could be an asset for your club as it heads into camp.

For more information on LJ, please feel free to drop me a line. Or you could contact his agent Mike O'Brien directly.

Best,
Ted Kluck

This week I call Parker before he calls me to make his weekly inquiry about pictures and game film. The truth of the matter is that without practice I'm kind of missing my teammates. We agree to meet in Grand Rapids for a lift at his old high school.

Parker rolls up in an old conversion van, the kind with drapes, swivel seats, and lots of leather. Rap music thumps out of the sound system and in the back are reams of laminated photos of Parker in various stages of football glory—high school, All-Star games, college, and beyond.

"I've got the merchandise," he says, handing me a stack of DVDs of all of our games, procured from Sean Lalonde. As a de-facto agent I will go about the business of burning copies of these to distribute to teams, including the San Diego Chargers if they are amenable. I've made it my goal to see that L.J., Rich, and Eric Gardner aren't destroying their bodies for peanuts next year.

We make our weekly call to Kubiak together, from L.J.'s van. We learn that for the fourth-consecutive week there is no practice, and we learn that one of our best defensive backs, who was mysteriously absent in Port Huron, was actually in jail for the weekend—pulled over en route for driving with a suspended license. "At least he wasn't trying to pimp us," says Bob, who sounds surprisingly upbeat in light of what he's been through.

We learn that L.J. will not be playing offense ("total bullshit"—his words) and that Chesaurae Rhodes is actually planning on playing this week after suffering the seizures just a week before. I am nonconfrontational by nature but I mention to Kubiak that maybe a guy with epilepsy shouldn't be playing a contact sport.

"I talked to him today," he says. "He's ready to go."

"How can I not be playing offense?" L.J. asks rhetorically as we dismount the van and make our way into the Ottawa Hills High School weight room. "I had three catches for 32 yards and Richard had six for thirty-nine. I averaged over 10 yards per catch."

Parker then gives me an impromptu tour of his high school. "This was my school," he says, opening the door to the gymnasium

where a large photograph of a state-champion basketball team fills
the back wall. "That's me, first player on your right in the back row."

We are met at the door by an unhappy women's basketball
coach–type, wearing a whistle around her neck and a scowl on her
face. She looks to be running an off-season practice or a basketball
camp of some kind.

"I'm gonna need to close these doors," she says, clearly unaware
of the fact that she had two real, live professional football players in
her presence. And unaware of the fact that this was once L. J.
Parker's school.

When I get home from the lift there is a response in my inbox from
Cam Cameron of the San Diego Chargers:

> *Ted, not a real surprise to me. L.J. has always had great talent. All he
> needed to do was mature. Sounds like he has. Give him my best. NFL?
> You never know. God Bless, Cam*

—————————————

> *Sent from my BlackBerry Wireless Handheld*

I also try, unsuccessfully, to play the game DVDs from Sean. I get
the message "no data" when I insert them into my DVD player and
my computer. The Intern gave us blank disks.

Chapter Eleven

Character

Game 10: Battle Creek Crunch versus NY/NJ Revolution

Driving to the arena with my dad I realize this is the last time I will wheel my car into the Kellogg Arena ramp, and the last time I'll drag my bag to the players' entrance in back. It's the last time I'll walk past all the junk in the back of the arena (junk in the back of arenas fascinates me . . . old seats and lights, for instance) and enter to find Doc Martinez in the throes of his latest crisis.

"I can't find my ice buckets, Teddy," he says as I enter. "How am I supposed to do my job without ice buckets?"

Pregame is just a long series of crisis. One of the Illegal Motion dancers has left her pompoms at home. She also lost her purse. Kyle Lacksheide has forgotten his socks and one of the Revolution players forgot his game jersey and is taken to a local mall by Sean Lalonde to get a replacement made up.

I learn that Doc Martinez actually wore a jersey to a local bookstore to make a last-minute "player-appearance" because there were no actual players available.

"I told them I played special teams," he says. "But my daughter kind of sold me out when she told one of the teachers that I was a chiropractor. But I still signed a bunch of autographs and read them a story."

We are joined by Coach Ashe who refers to my dad politely as Mr. Kluck and tells a story about how he had to drive to Detroit and rent vans for the Revolution players to get them from the airport to the arena.

"I don't even bring my wallet anymore," he says. "I was supposed to get five thousand dollars for this coaching deal and I'm already about six thousand dollars in the hole. When I went to rent the cars the lady asked for my driver's license and everything and told me I would have to drive both cars. I said, 'Lady I'm no PhD but I think that's impossible.'"

Everybody laughs. Scott Ashe is as skilled a storyteller as I've met in any walk of life.

The Revolution players have already trickled out onto the field (no new turf) to toss footballs around. Many of them look different; it seems that the Revs have turned over about half of their roster since their last trip to Battle Creek. New Revs quarterback Julio Ramirez sidles up to the wall. He looks old, probably mid- to late-thirties, as do several of the Revs. I ask him about the trip.

"I'm really glad we flew," he says, "because the bus rides were getting dangerous. Our last ride up to Rochester we designated one guy to stay awake with the driver to keep him up. While the rest of the guys were knocked out in back of the bus I was up there giving this guy energy drinks and coffee. But he was still closing his eyes! I said. 'Man, pull over.' And I threw some water on him and bought him some Jolt. But I think it got to the point where we had over-caffeinated him and he was falling asleep from that."

I compliment him and his team for their positive attitudes and classy play, even though they have lost all of their games, all on the road.

"This is fun for me," he says. "I work for a maintenance company in the city and several years ago I had the chance to go to school and play out in Arizona but it was too far away, man. I would have gotten homesick so I just stayed here and did this, to be close to my family.

"You know, when we were checking in to get our rental cars and told the lady we played professional football she said, 'You know, you guys really seem to like each other, and you seem to have a lot more fun than the NFL guys.'"

As the hours and minutes tick away before game time I am encouraged to see the majority of my teammates walk through the door—

Lacksheide (looking ridiculous in CHIPS-style aviator sunglasses), T.P., Eric Gardner, Gills, Parker, and Ches. Ches's participation has been a hot topic of conversation today. Will he or won't he play? Is it or isn't it a good idea? But as Ches finally enters the locker room, Lacksheide breaks the tension by yelling out: "Hey everybody, Twitchy is here!" A week ago the guy was laying on some bad Astroturf fighting for his life, now he is back in the locker room being ridiculed again.

"I thought you was dancing," says L. J. Parker of the initial moments Ches spent on the turf in Port Huron. "I told you to get your ass up. You remember that?"

"I wanted to but I couldn't move," says Ches earnestly, in reply. "I missed you guys," he continues, in response to the shouts of "Twitch."

I pull a Kinkos bag out from beneath my seat and grab the large, glossy picture of Ches that I had printed for him, courtesy of Jim Olson. It is the quintessential Chesaurae shot—he is dancing, orange bandanna and orange spats in the air, to "Thank God I'm a Country Boy" during a time-out at our last home game. I made similar pics for Gills, Gardner, and a few other players and coaches. Making the photos—picking the shots that best exemplified my teammates—was one of the most satisfying experiences of my season.

"This is really nice, Ted," he says, staring at his own image on paper. It is, besides some stolen equipment (we're all keeping our gear, in lieu of paychecks), all that he will take away from this experience as proof that it actually existed. "I really appreciate this," he says again, before wandering out into the concourse to show the photo to his wife.

Today's pregame has a last-day-of-camp feel about it. Players are as relaxed and buoyant as we were morose and uptight last week. Lacksheide has a football that he's circulating around for signatures—most of which involve references to Lack's girth in some context or another.

"Who were you going to give that to?" asks Richard Gills, as he scrawls the words "Fat Ass" on Lack's football.

"My grandma, but I guess that's out," Lacksheide replies, looking a little down. We're all in souvenir mode now, desperate to leave with proof of our existence as pro football players because it looks less and less likely that the Battle Creek Crunch will exist next season.

It also appears that the days of eating free Hungry Howie's pizza in the locker room before the game are over. There are no pizzas in the locker room and my dad and I, with Tom Mack, go on a search for candy bars in the arena lobby. On our way back we pass a makeshift apparel stand, where an Illegal Motion dancer is selling what remains of the Crunch T-shirts and sweatshirts.

"How much are the T-shirts?" I ask her, hoping that she'll help a couple of players out with freebies.

"Fifteen dollars," she replies.

"But since you're a player I'll give you one for fifteen dollars," my dad jokes, as we walk away. He then asks T-Mack if he plans on playing next season.

"Nope, this is definitely it for me," he replies. "I'm thirty-three years old and my kids are nine and six so now it's their time."

Midway through the second quarter we are up by a tidy sum (17–0 I believe) and I am summoned to work on the kickoff team. Herb Haygood shakes his fist at me—"Make the tackle, Kluck," he says. "Hit somebody!"

I jog out onto the hard green turf next to L. J. Parker who is smiling behind the bars of his face mask. I ask Parker where he wants me to line up.

"Right by me," he says.

"Nice job on that kick return," says Lacksheide in the locker room at halftime. I know that he is about to say something derisive because my first kickoff wasn't a nice job. I lost sight of the ballcarrier after being hit hard by a Revs blocker.

"You got spun around like a top," he adds.

"Thanks for noticing," I reply.

The game firmly in hand, there is no drama in the halftime locker room, save for the fact that Lacksheide, who played the first half with no socks, now has a raging case of blisters.

The second half offers more opportunities for me to play on the kickoff and kick return teams. Jersey scores twice in the third quarter to keep it interesting, but a 1-yard run by Tim Kubiak (Timmy's runs are, by far, the ugliest I have ever seen in football) and a nice 40-yard fade to Richard Gills keeps us comfortably in front. After the Revs' second touchdown, I am summoned to play on the kickoff return team and line up on the front row. My job, usually, would be to peel back and retreat, hoping to set up a wedge and "pick off" a Revs defender on the way back.

"Don't peel back this time," says Tom Mack, who will line up next to me on the front line. "Just pick the guy in front of you and go get him."

The guy in front of me is Eddie Chan, the Revs' All-Star linebacker, who at 6-foot-1 and 230 pounds could start for any team in the league. At the kick, I sprint up and hit Chan as hard as I can, straight on. The collision rattles me, but it feels good. I feel a throbbing pain in my arm and neck.

With 1:45 remaining in the third quarter, I get perhaps the biggest thrill of the season. I line up next to Richard Gills and Shaun Blackmon in the end zone and race downfield to cover the Brad Selent kick, as I have before. Selent booms a perfect shot down into the corner of the NY/NJ end zone, where Anthony Reece fields the ball and turns upfield. I successfully evade a block attempt by Rich Martucci (who hit me right in the throat on the previous kickoff— this hurts) and weave my way through traffic, finding myself incredibly close to Reece, who has made a cut to the left around the 10-yard line. I close in on him with Shaun Blackmon, feeling my arms wrap around his torso, and my shoulder driving into the small of his back. I see Richard Gills's face as we untangle the pile. "Yeah, Kluck!" he says, as we jog off. I have made a tackle. I'm in the record books. I'm a statistic.

Chapter Twelve

The Last Picture Show

Weeks since our last practice: ten

Wheeling the Echo into the Olivet College football complex for practice feels almost like a new experience again. I have Mike O'Brien with me and he is trying to sign Eric Gardner to a representation contract because E.G. is a two-way star and leading candidate for MVP of the league. O'Brien feels that Gardner has the potential to play in the AFL, or perhaps even the NFL, where safeties with his size and speed are a rarity. If only he could track him down.

"I called the cell number he gave me after the game and it said the number was no longer in service," he tells me, as if this is a new revelation. E.G. is somewhat legendary in team circles for changing his telephone number.

As we're walking into the facility, Herb Haygood wheels his tricked-out Cadillac SUV into the parking lot. While not ostentatious necessarily, it is a car that definitely says, "I played in the league." Yet, in not too many years, it will be a reminder of how long it has been since he played in the league. And a few years after that it will be scrap metal, just like the rest of us.

We enter to find Gills, Parker, and Gardner lounging in the lobby. Gardner is wearing a Texas Rangers cap placed strategically at a sideways angle, and shorts falling halfway down his ass as is customary. The players each give me the obligatory pro athlete hug. I've also found myself using their words and phrases in my everyday life. I'll probably need to break myself of that habit in a couple of weeks, when I am no longer a pro football player but again just a guy.

Practice starts in a half hour and there are only a handful of players present. O'Brien gives Gardner a quick spiel, and then asks

E.G. to write his phone numbers on a tablet. He is writing for several minutes.

"Good thing I brought a lot of paper," O'Brien quips.

The players are giving E.G. the business because he missed our last road game in Port Huron because of back spasms, but was photographed in a local newspaper the next morning playing in a celebrity softball game. They are less concerned with his lack of participation in the Port Huron game, and more concerned that he may have referred to himself as a celebrity.

"You a celebrity?" Gills asks.

Gardner smiles a sly grin. I have never seen him upset, or even mildly temperamental, as opposed to Gills and Parker whose moods swing with regularity. "I'm big in K-Zoo baby, that's my town," he replies. "I got me a base hit and then sat on the bench for the rest of the game." There is not a hint of guile, or guilt, in his voice. It is E.G. being E.G.

Ken Kubiak enters the locker room and begins introducing himself to everyone—a poke at the fact that we haven't practiced in weeks.

I get a quick prepractice lift in before the players trickle out to the field. It will probably be my last lift in this facility, provided we lose to Port Huron this weekend in the opening game of the GLIFL playoffs. There are some Olivet college players lifting, and the same, familiar songs are pounding out of the sound system—"Welcome to the Jungle," Thunderstruck," ad infinitum. The same songs I lifted to ten years ago. The players stalk around wordlessly, just as they did a decade ago. Nothing changes in football.

On the field, the mood is somber; only nine players have shown up.

"I can't believe I drove four hours back from Traverse City for this," says Ashe, looking around at the small group of players. "What are we going to do with ten guys?"

Kyle Lacksheide and TP are lying on their backs, on the artificial FieldTurf surface. TP, per usual, has his hand down his shorts, adjusting his junk.

"It smells like rubber down here," says TP, flicking the small pieces of ground-up tire that lie between the blades of artificial green turf.

They engage Ashe in a discussion of northern Michigan bars (places with names like "The Bucksnort") and compare notes on where they have or haven't been in fistfights. I would like to hear more about these stories but being a part of these discussions means never acting shocked by anything. There is a requisite cool indifference that comes with being a football player.

Practice is expectedly sluggish, but with a handful of players in uniform, we are able to put in a new run package to use against Port Huron, which will feature Eric Gardner running the option. Gardner, however, apparently lost his helmet after the last game.

"One of those little league kids stole it," he says, of a group of kids from Ohio who visited Kellogg Arena for our last home game and spent the postgame trolling the field looking for cast-off equipment. "They were like vultures."

Gardner is padding up in Ken Kubiak's helmet and shoulder pads, which look big and ridiculous on him. "I feel like a peewee kid," he says, adjusting the large helmet. Kubiak just shakes his head and looks at me.

"You and me man, constantly taking it for the team," he says. "Welcome to pro football."

Gardner's equipment problems give me the chance to line up at tailback, running several toss plays against our defense in a half-line scrimmage. For the first time I get to experience what it feels like for a running back to try to make his way through the line with a defense hurtling itself full-speed in his direction. It is a harrowing experience to say the least. Before I know it, I am around the corner—thanks to a hook block by Pettaway—and tightroping up the sidelines before being blasted out of bounds by Parker. I see his dark eyes, widened behind the metal face mask, focusing on me before he delivers the hit.

My body feels surprisingly good, save for chronically sore shoulders that are more a result of years of weight lifting and other seasons of football than any particular pounding I've taken this year. The sore shoulders often wake me up at night, and I've taken to slathering them with Flexall, which smells oddly of peppermint and Pepto-Bismol.

In the huddle I notice Tim Kubiak's badly swollen right elbow, encircled by a nasty purplish bruise. My respect level for Kubiak has skyrocketed this season. He has deftly handled criticism from team-mates and the media and steadily improved his game.

"I was 250 pounds at the first tryout," he told me, when asked about his decision to play again this season. "Bob said to just lose 20, so I started running and got down to 230. Now I feel great."

Kubiak is struggling today though, because his elbow—swollen to the size of a softball—is killing him. We are joined halfway through practice by a black kid, a new DB, wearing a tight red Under Armour shirt and NFL gloves. He is an assistant basketball coach at Olivet College who played professional indoor ball with Sioux Falls in the United Indoor League this season. He also, apparently, isn't aware of end-of-the-season etiquette, and is jawing relentlessly at Kubiak—telling him not to lob any junk his way. In college, we called guys like this "Thursday's All-American," meaning that they were great in practice, in shorts, when it didn't matter.

"Gills, run a fade on this f—ker," says Kubiak to Gills in the hud-dle. "And get open."

At the break we move to the line of scrimmage. Kubiak takes the shotgun snap from Lacksheide and drifts back into the pocket, loft-ing a perfect spiral over the head of Thursday's All-American, and into the hands of Gills streaking 30 yards down the right sideline. Gills never breaks stride, his gloved hands gathering the ball out of a perfectly cool evening sky.

"I just talked to coach," says L. J. Parker, on the other end of my cell phone. I can tell by the tone of his voice that he's pissed. "I was ask-ing him when we're going to get paid," he continues.

"When are we going to get paid?" I ask.

"He said he told the league that we're not playing unless he gets the money in his hands before the start of the game," he continues. "And then he told me that he's not paying us until we all turn in our equipment at the end of the game. He said when he gets our helmets and jerseys, then he'll give us the money."

I take a moment to envision that ugly scene.

"I'm keeping my gear," Parker tells me in no uncertain terms. "I've been playing the whole season for nothing, basically. What's another two hundred bucks at this point? I'd rather have my helmet and jerseys."

We both agree that we're not even taking our black home jerseys on the trip. If they want those they can come after them later. And I already have a spot cleared off on my desk for the black Crunch helmet which, in all likelihood, will end up being worn by Eric Gardner in tomorrow's game.

"It's been a crappy day," Parker continues. He has had his hours cut down to one day at the Longhorn Steakhouse, where he is a grill cook. The football money, insignificant as it may seem, is important to him.

Playoffs, Game 1: Battle Creek versus Port Huron

I think the saying is something like, "Déjà vu all over again." The fact of the matter is that we lost, again, to Port Huron, 74–3 in much the same fashion that we lost the first game. It sucked. It hurt. Rayshawn Askew scored about a zillion touchdowns, and we got beat, man up, at nearly every position. While we were wondering if our players would even show up, Port Huron's brass was concerned with such things as flying star players in from Florida and getting the players their contracted allotment of free meals. The two teams exist in very different worlds.

I find Doc Martinez first, limping through the locker room with a vacant look in his eye. I can tell something is wrong.

"I had a bad week, Teddy," he says. "My son left for home early— said he wanted to be with his friends, I found out that I can't see Amanda any more, and then I hurt my shoulder."

Doc can barely lift his right arm, and eventually puts the hurt limb into a sling. His son, Chance (also our best water boy), left for Kansas, where he lives with his mother.

"On Friday after my boy left," he says, "I just curled up into a ball and cried. I couldn't move. My ex-wife told Sean before she left to not let me do anything to myself, because Chance would never forgive himself."

Only another parent understands what it feels like to say good-bye to a child. I recount to Doc how it felt when we were adopting Tristan, and the Ukrainian government said after our first two trips to his country that we had to go home to America and wait it out. We had to, essentially, leave our son in a cold, dank orphanage. I have never cried like that, before or since. It was unbridled anger mixed with the disappointment and the fear that only a parent knows.

I think about Tristan, two miles up the road in a hotel, waiting for me to get back home. I opted to keep them at the hotel tonight, rather than have them suffer through another game, in another hostile arena, alone. Especially this arena with its belligerent fans and loud pirate impersonators.

My hope for tonight is for a healthy game for L.J., Richard, Gardner, myself, and the rest of our guys. And except for the regular pounding one takes in a football game, L.J. and Gardner will make it through fine. Now they can focus on the business of getting faster and stronger for the AFL tryouts in the fall. Richard, however, isn't so lucky. He twists his knee in a pileup in the second quarter, after a stellar first quarter in which he single-handedly moved our offense on quick slants and hooks. The big receiver hobbles to the sidelines where Doc begins manipulating the knee.

The game offers other unique story lines. One is our center Kyle Lacksheide, for the first time all season, being completely dominated. Lack has been an alpha male the entire year—laughing and taunting his way to an All-Star selection, but tonight he is mentally and physically destroyed by Pirates NT Ed Bausley.

Bausley has set up residence inside Lack's shaven head, causing him to fire two shotgun snaps over Tim Kubiak's head, resulting in Port Huron safeties. Usually a constant source of trash talk and banter, Lacksheide is eerily silent on the sidelines, no doubt pondering what it feels like to be, perhaps for the first time in his life, on the receiving end of a beating. The halftime score is 39–3, Port Huron.

At halftime the locker room is like a morgue. Players are morose, wondering how we will survive another thirty minutes of football, and wondering whether Port Huron will score 100 points—something that has happened a handful of times in these minor indoor leagues. An all-travel team called the Carolina Ghostriders got 100 points hung on them last year. It's something nobody wants to think about.

Meanwhile, Richard Gills is beside himself, trying to jog and jump on a painful knee that isn't responding. He has spent the last several weeks excitedly talking with Mike O'Brien about the future— about workouts, letters to AFL teams, and the like. Now, with one play, that future has become extremely murky for a kid with a bum knee and no health insurance. He sits alone, with a silent Doc Martinez, and cries. They are two men with problems.

Bob Kubiak has another problem and its name is Rick Radcliffe, director of officials for the GLIFL. Radcliffe made the unfortunate decision to come into our locker room to talk to Kubiak about a call his crew made early in the second quarter—an illegal chop block call which negated a touchdown that would have kept us in the ball game. The Tim Kubiak touchdown pass to Herb Haygood was called back after tackle Tyler Paesens allegedly "cut blocked" his man outside of an imaginary "box" around the line of scrimmage where such a block is legal. The rule, as with most GLIFL rules this season, is confusing to say the least.

To put it nicely, Bob Kubiak is tearing this guy a new one, using every word in an extensive arsenal of profanity. Kubiak's assertion, and it's a good one, is that there's a new set of rules every week.

They are standing in a small room near the showers, and through an open door sits the team, listening to every word. Also listening to this tirade in the same room are our ball boys, quietly eating free sub sandwiches and Gatorade as though all of this was no big deal. Finally, Scott Ashe's voice is heard booming from the other room.

"Bob, get his ass out of here!"

And just like that Radcliffe is gone. Kubiak returns and tells us to be professional. Play hard. Don't get down on each other. He berates Chesaurae Rhodes for something he didn't do in the first half. Ches was accused of pointing fingers on the sideline when he was actually just talking to Doc about a bruised knee.

Most of our star players did show up, and we still got pounded, which in many ways makes it worse than it was before because there were fewer excuses this time. Their players danced and preened all over the field and instead of shaking hands at the end, I just beat it. I wanted to be in the locker room with my friends, with our guys because those are the things I'll miss. I'll miss eating pizza in the locker room after games. I'll miss the feeling of leaving the locker room with a wet head after the postgame shower, rolling my bag past the lingering fans on the way out to the car, knowing they're looking at me because I'm a Player. I'll never have that again.

There is some sentimentality in the locker room, as Coach Kubiak closes the door and we all sit around, half undressed. He lauds us for finishing the year, courageously, despite not getting paid. He tells us to go ahead and take our jerseys, which is a class move. He says that he has never been around a classier group of guys. I look around the room at Parker and Gills, next to me, Ches getting dressed in the corner, and Kubiak and Allsbury with the rest of the MAC guys in back. Thursday's All-American dresses alone. He got beat like a drum tonight.

"I just want to tell you guys that I had a blast this season," says Pettaway. He is in his mid-thirties, and is probably at something of a life crossroads. He had the least trouble doing this for free because he is a successful pharmaceutical rep, and because he's been playing semipro football for nothing, for years. "You guys are all class."

The one unrelenting reality of football is that if you are reading this, chances are you are looking (or will look) at the game through the rearview mirror. Football is a sport without a future, which I guess is what makes it so special. There are no rec leagues for old guys and no Saturday morning runs at the Y. If you're lucky your window closes without much drama and they don't have to carry you off on a stretcher.

For most it means just being able to watch a game without being insanely jealous of the young men playing. If you can catch a Big Ten game at the stadium or watch *Monday Night Football* without hating the guys on the field, or obsessing about how much younger than you they are, there is hope. There is hope if you can watch a game without sizing everyone up and deciding which guys are "about your size" or "more or less as athletic" than you are.

The key, I suppose is to get out before anyone begins feeling sorry for you.

Allsbury kisses his Crunch helmet and chucks it in a pile that has formed in the middle of the locker room floor.

Kenny Kubiak, who gave me a GLIFL football at the end of the game, tells me to send it around the room for signatures. I dig through my bag, only to find that the ball has already been stolen by one of my teammates, hungry for a souvenir. It is a quintessential Crunch moment. Nothing is sacred.

There are more tributes voiced, and finally Kyle Lacksheide stands up.

"I just want you guys to know that I had a great time playing with you all and getting to know you this season," he says. The room, mostly quiet, nods its approval until finally, Tyler Paesens raises a hand to speak.

"F—k you, Lacksheide," he says. The place cracks up.

I say goodbye to Doc and give him a hug, promising to call him next week. I do the same for L.J. and Richard, and after opening the heavy steel door I am alone outside in a dark, humid Port Huron night. The lights from the carnival next door are reflected in the door of my car, and I realize that if I get back to the hotel quickly, I'll be able to tuck my son into bed.

The Tryout, 2006

The television is the size of a small country, and engulfs the living room of Eric Gardner's sister. The characters on screen (from an unfortunate Jim Brown movie circa the seventies) are almost life size. I am chatting with Eric's mother, who is pretending that a life-sized Jim Brown over my shoulder isn't dodging bullets or blowing up a tanker truck while we're trying to converse. It's a little distracting. She's telling me about all of the NFL players that Eric knew as a kid in Kalamazoo—guys like T. J. Duckett, Greg Jennings, Jerome Harrison, Charles Rogers.

"I just don't understand why none of them have helped Eric out," she says, sadly, before Jim Brown pops another cap in another bad guy just over my left shoulder.

I'm in Kalamazoo to pick up Eric and transport him to Grand Rapids for a private workout with the Grand Rapids Rampage of the AFL. Eric informed me last night, at midnight, that he would be unable to get himself to the workout, so I drove out of my way to deliver him. The Rampage have invited me to try out as well, so this may be the last time I pull on a pair of gloves and cleats, and get to run around on a football field. This, after the last last time.

Gardner climbs into my Pontiac Vibe and settles in amidst the coloring books, toy cars, and other parental detritus. I wonder what he thinks of it. When Eric Gardner drives, he drives a champagne-colored Cadillac.

"You nervous, E.G.?" I ask him, after a few moments of football chit-chat.

"Naw man . . . don't get nervous . . . I haven't been nervous since the tenth grade," he says through heavy eyelids, before leaning his seat back and succumbing to sleep. His omnipresent cell phone vibrates a total of seventeen times during the fifty-five minute trip. Eric Gardner is a popular guy. I learn, before he falls asleep, that he has lived in Mississippi and Los Angeles, where his junior college regularly scrimmaged with USC and UCLA.

We are greeted at "The Soccer Spot" in Kentwood, Michigan, by Rampage coaches Michael Baker and Tom Riva. Baker, a former AFL star player will work Gardner out, and Riva will put me through the paces. I make sure Riva has been briefed on my status as an author-player, to stave off any anger over getting out of bed to work out a guy who has little to no chance of every making his club.

E.G. is run through a variety of agility and ball drills, and looks athletic and competent, as is usual for him. Midway through the workout, however, he leaves the field and disappears into the bathroom for several minutes.

"He's puking," says Baker, with a smile from the other end of the field, clearly enjoying it.

Meanwhile, I am put through a variety of agility drills by Riva, who keeps me entertained and relaxed with a steady stream of banter the entire time. He coached in Europe as well as on the Indiana small-college circuit, and as it turns out we know a lot of the same people. Riva teaches me pass blocking techniques, while explaining that the arena game features the "purest of all line play," because there is very little allowed in the way of stunts. Each play is one-on-one, man-on-man blocking.

Gardner returns from his bathroom hiatus to finish the workout, while Riva and I are still going strong. It makes me feel good to know that I was able to finish without falling out.

On our way out of the building we meet briefly with Sparky McEwen, the Rampage head coach. He has a severe mustache and gives me a more-solid-than-necessary coach handshake. McEwen clearly isn't here to banter.

"You need to get in better shape," he tells Gardner. "But we saw some great things that you brought to the table. We'd like to work you out again in November. The key to these private workouts, Eric, is being in top condition and being ready to roll at all times. But I know it's hard with kids, a job, and a family."

Gardner nods at all the right times, and promises to get into better shape. I'm proud of him, and I hope it works out for him. McEwen eyes me for a moment at the end of the meeting.

"Riva took it easy on you," he says. I don't know whether it's appropriate to chuckle right now, but I do anyway. "But he also said you're a good athlete. You did real well."

Over mall-food-court Chinese food a couple of weeks after the season, Doc Martinez tells me the sordid tale of the hours that followed our playoff loss to Port Huron. His left eye is a ghoulish shade of purple and the eyeball itself is still bloodshot. I ask him to describe the evening.

He and Sean Lalonde are hanging out with new DE Chris Roberson and several other players—both Crunch and Pirates players—at the house of a friend in the wee hours of the morning. The coaches are there, too, and they stage an impromptu foot race in the street outside the house, timing drunken players as they wobble down the street. The cops come and go twice. Much booze is consumed, words are exchanged, and Doc (wearing a sling at the time for his shoulder impingement) is sucker-punched in the face by a Port Huron Pirates linebacker, who is roughly twice Doc's size. The player, it turns out, was supposedly in the face of the party's hostess, calling her all manner of unflattering things. There was also, allegedly, contact.

"You don't hit a girl, Teddy," Doc tells me. "I was defending her honor." On the way out of the mall we are approached by a couple of his patients. "Hi, Doc!" they say, with a wave.

"I love that," he explains. "Nobody would ever call me 'Doc' back home, because of all the history. But I worked hard for that. I worked hard to be called 'Doc'."

Doc will be hitting the road with a professional wrestling circuit, acting as their ringside physician, next week. Drama, it seems, never stops following him.

L. J. Parker, Richard Gills, and Eric Gardner have all signed representation agreements with Mike O'Brien, and he has supplied them with workout manuals the size of New York City phone books, to aide them in their off-season training. He ran into an NFL player last week who played high school ball with Eric Gardner and said he was the best athlete he'd ever seen. True to form, he is finding Eric Gardner difficult to get a hold of. His last number had been disconnected. L.J. Parker, on the other hand, made the most of an open tryout with the AFL's Grand Rapids Rampage, and was signed to a training camp contract. He was the first GLIFL player to sign with the big league.

After he plays in the GLIFL All-Star game, Herb Haygood will report to Olivet College, where he will serve as an assistant coach, overseeing the wide receivers.

Ken Kubiak will join his brother Bob on the Olivet coaching staff, handling the defensive backs, and Tim Kubiak will return to Kalamazoo, where he will teach middle school mathematics. Ken, it should be noted, has retired at age thirty-nine from professional football.

Bob Kubiak called me a couple of days ago to say that he had a two-hundred-dollar game check from the playoffs for me, which I thought was a class move. He has added "instructor" to his list of duties at Olivet College; he will be teaching a class this fall. He is, in his words, spending "way too much time" fielding calls from people to whom the Battle Creek Crunch organization owes money. He just wants to coach football.

Tyler Paesens is still running things at the Garfield Lake Tavern in Olivet, and Kyle Lacksheide is still drinking there regularly in addition to framing houses, finishing school, and marketing his services to AFL and NFL clubs.

Harry Pettaway is still a pharmaceutical rep, and Scott Ashe a principal at Napoleon High School near Jackson, Michigan.

Chesaurae Rhodes is tending bar in Detroit, and playing RB for the Detroit Seminoles, one of the nation's premier semipro outfits. Most important, though, he is healthy, and has signed a contract to play for the GLIFL's Marion Mayhem next season.

Azriel Woodson, "The Preacher," is also playing with the Seminoles, with Carmell Dennis, while he trains for one last shot at professional football. He is engaged to be married next summer, and has now played for four professional indoor franchises.

Chuck Selinger called me recently to let me know that if I needed anyone with "writing acumen" to proofread my manuscript, that he was available. He also let me know that he is considering approaching some of the new expansion clubs in the league—in Detroit and Muskegon—but would only kick for them if they had stable "long snapping and holding situations." Selinger, apparently, failed to learn that nothing is stable at this level.

Crunch kicker Brad Selent, who kicked very well for us this season, is considering another tryout with the Grand Rapids Rampage.

Brian Dolph has recovered well from a fractured knee and elbow, and has been volunteering with a local high school team in addition to his work as a financial advisor. He plans on playing for the Crunch next year.

Sean Lalonde, Crunch GM, has been interviewing for indoor football front office jobs around the Midwest, but has yet to find a fit. He is currently rooming with Doc Martinez.

Mike Powell, wisely, has disappeared. He has become a regular person. He will go down as the first, and only, owner of the Battle Creek Crunch. The team is now, officially, defunct.

They say you can never go back, but I'm trying. My son, now age four, just got his first bike for his birthday and he is pedaling it around my old high school, in Hartford City. It feels like it's about 110 degrees outside, and I can smell a mixture of burned grass, cornfields, local farms, and the high school practice field. I am overcome by nostalgia. I walk down to the cleat house building, to get a glimpse of the place where I dressed for practices and games every summer and fall for four years. The football field and cleat house look exactly the same. Nothing has changed.

As I make my way around the high school building with Tristan and my dad, I stop to look in the glass windows. The industrial arts wing. The band room. The language arts wing. I want very badly, all of a sudden, to go inside.

"Wanna run some routes?" Dad asks, digging an official GLIFL game ball out of the trunk of the car. I gave him the ball after one of our early season games.

I haven't played a game in three weeks. The last time I touched a football was in the locker room, after the last Port Huron game, getting autographs. My cleats are stiff and I am wearing an old pair of receiver's gloves because frankly, they make me feel cool. I limber up with a few long fly patterns, jogging easily under the lazy lobs, my workout shorts swishing as I run. This is good. It is satisfying like opening a present early or ordering a pizza at the exact moment that you see the advertisement on television.

"Gimmie a 15-yard out," he says.

I dig my cleats into the hard turf. We are playing on a high school practice field. There are some kids on a soccer field nearby. Ever the narcissist, I wonder what they think of me. Do they think I'm pathetic for trying to recapture a little bit of lost youth? I settle into my three-point stance and can feel the hot, burned Indiana grass through my gloves.

At the signal I take off, sprinting to the imaginary spot 15 yards downfield where I will make my break. I reach the spot and settle into the familiar athletic crouch, cutting sharply to the right. According to coaches and conventional football wisdom, this is where "separation" is created and the receiver creates space between himself and the defensive back. I whip my head around and catch a glimpse of my father following through, watching me run.

The ball is in the air.

Battle Creek Crunch Roster

#/POS	PLAYER NAME	HT	WT	EXPERIENCE
2/WR/DB	Chesaurae Rhodes	5' 8"	185	Ten. Valley (UIF)
3/WR/DB	Shawn Blackmon	6' 1"	225	Semipro
4/WR/DB	Richard Gills IV	6' 4"	225	Northwood
5/WR/LB	L. J. Parker	6' 2"	235	Indiana
7/QB	Tim Kubiak	6' 2"	225	Toledo
10/WR/DB	Eric Gardner	6' 1"	220	Olivet
13/FB/LB	Azriel Woodson	6' 1"	235	UIF
14/QB	Ken Kubiak	6' 2"	215	Olivet
15/OL/DL	Brian Wright	6' 3"	265	Semipro
18/K	Brad Selent	6' 0"	200	Detroit (AFL)
27/WR/DB	Herb Haygood	6' 1"	215	Michigan State
37/DL/LB	Anthony Allsbury	6' 2"	265	Western Michigan
61/OL/DL	Kyle Lackscheide	6' 3"	300	Olivet
65/OL/DL	Kevin Smith	6' 3"	265	Semipro
78/OL/DL	Kevin Kramer	6' 3"	300	Western Michigan
92/OL/DL	Harry Pettaway	6' 2"	295	Western Michigan
95/OL/DL	Tyler Paesens	6' 5"	365	Olivet, Wayne State
25/LS	Ted Kluck	6' 2"	225	Taylor (IN)
Practice/IR				
FB-LB	Dawaynne Thompson			
FB-LB	Will Warren	6' 0"	265	USMC
RB/LB	Carmell Dennis	6' 2"	260	Carson-Newman
DB	Delano Harry	6' 0"	205	Wayne State
WR/DB	Brian Dolph	6' 3"	210	Indiana (AFL)

Ted Kluck is a freelance writer whose work appears regularly on ESPN.com and in the pages of *Sports Spectrum* magazine where his column, *Pro and Con*, received a national award in 2003. His first book, *Facing Tyson*, was published in 2006 by the Lyons Press. He lives in Lansing, Michigan, with wife, Kristin, and son, Tristan, and will never play football again.